Aristotle's Criticism of Plato's *Republic*

Aristotle's Criticism of Plato's *Republic*

ROBERT MAYHEW

ROWMAN & LITTLEFIELD PUBLISHERS, INC.
Lanham • Boulder • New York • Oxford

ROWMAN & LITTLEFIELD PUBLISHERS, INC.

Published in the United States of America
by Rowman & Littlefield Publishers, Inc.
4720 Boston Way, Lanham, Maryland 20706

12 Hid's Copse Road
Cummor Hill, Oxford OX2 9JJ, England

This book is based on a 1991 doctoral dissertation for Georgetown University.

British Library Cataloguing in Publication Information Available

Library of Congress Cataloging-in-Publication Data

Mayhew, Robert.
    Aristotle's criticism of Plato's Republic / Robert Mayhew.
      p. cm.
    Includes bibliographical references and indexes.
    ISBN 0-8476-8654-X (alk. paper). — ISBN 0-8476-8655-8 (pbk. : alk. paper)
    1. Aristotle. Politics. 2. Plato. Republic. I. Title.
JC71.A7M39 1997
320.1'01—dc21   97-20980
                                                       CIP

ISBN: 978-0-8476-8655-1

Printed in the United States of America

To Estelle

Contents

Preface

The first five chapters of the second book of Aristotle's *Politics* contain a series of criticisms leveled against Plato's *Republic*. Given the importance of Plato and Aristotle in the history of political philosophy, it is surprising that despite the abundance of work on Aristotle's *Politics*, these chapters have for the most part been neglected. For instance, there has been no book-length study of them written this century. This is an unfortunate gap in Aristotelian scholarship—one that I hope here to make a contribution toward filling.

This book is not intended for specialists in Aristotle alone, but for anyone interested in the history of political thought. All passages from the Greek have been translated into English (by me, except where indicated). I have used Dreizehnter's edition of Aristotle's *Politics* and the Oxford Classical Text editions of Plato's *Republic* and Aristotle's *Nicomachean Ethics*. I often consulted Lord's translation of the *Politics*, Irwin's and Ross's translations of the *Nicomachean Ethics*, and Bloom's and Grube's translations of the *Republic*.

Some of the material in this book has appeared elsewhere, though all of it was reworked in order to be incorporated into this book. Chapter 2 made use of "Part and Whole in Aristotle's Political Philosophy," *Journal of Ethics* (Kluwer Academic Publishers © 1997). Chapter 3 made use of "Aristotle on the Self-Sufficiency of the City," *History of Political Thought* (Imprint Academic © 1995). Chapter 4 made use of "Aristotle's Criticism of Plato's Communism of Women and Children," *Apeiron* (Academic Printing and Publishing © 1996), and "Impiety and Political Unity: Aristotle, *Politics* 1262a25-32," *Classical Philology* (The University of Chicago Press © 1996). Chapter 5 made use of "Aristotle on Property," *Review of Metaphysics* (*Review of Metaphysics* © 1993) and "The Communism of Property: A Note on Aristotle, *Politics* 1263a8-15," *Classical Quarterly* (Oxford University Press © 1995). The appendix appeared earlier as "Aristotle on the Extent of the Communism of Plato's *Republic*" in *Ancient Philosophy* (Mathesis Publications © 1993). (These articles are all being used here with the permission of the copyright holders.)

This book grew out of my doctoral dissertation (Department of Philosophy, Georgetown University, 1991). I owe a great deal to my two readers, Henry Richardson and Gerald Mara, and especially to the director of the dissertation, Alfonso Gomez-Lobo. I have also benefited from the comments, criticisms, and advice of a number of others who read all or part of some version(s) of this book, most importantly: Allan Gotthelf, Fred D. Miller, Jr., Anthony Preus, Peter Simpson, and Nicholas D. Smith. Special thanks to the Social Philosophy and Policy Center (Bowling Green State University), where I spent the summer of 1994 as a Visiting Scholar completing an earlier draft of this book, and to Seton Hall University for release time which helped me complete the final draft. Thanks also to Robin Adler, Dorothy Bradley and Lynn Weber at Rowman & Littlefield for all of their help on this project.

Finally, and most of all, thanks to my wife Estelle for constantly coming to the aid of her computer-ignorant husband, and for much more than I could possibly do justice to here.

Abbreviations

Aristophanes

Eccl.	*Ecclesiazusae*

Aristotle

AC	*Athenian Constitution*
Cat.	*Categories*
DA	*De Anima*
DC	*De Caelo*
DM	*De Mundo*
EE	*Eudemian Ethics*
GA	*Generation of Animals*
GC	*Generation and Corruption*
HA	*History of Animals*
MM	*Magna Moralia*
Met.	*Metaphysics*
Meteor.	*Meteorology*
NE	*Nicomachean Ethics*
Oec.	*Oeconomica*
PA	*Parts of Animals*
Phys.	*Physics*
Poet.	*Poetics*
Pol.	*Politics*
Probl.	*Problems*
Rhet.	*Rhetoric*
SE	*Sophistici Elenchi*
Top.	*Topics*

Plato

Rep.	*Republic*
Tim.	*Timaeus*

Xenophon

Hell.	*Hellenica*
LC	*Lakedaimonian Constitution*
Mem.	*Memoribilia*
Oec.	*Oeconomica*

Chapter One

Introduction

I do not agree with Plato, but if anything could make me do so, it would be
Aristotle's arguments against him.
  Bertrand Russell, *A History of Western Philosophy*

Scholarship on *Politics* II 1-5

Aristotle's *Politics* II 1-5 contains a series of criticisms leveled against
Plato's *Republic*. Surprisingly, these chapters have for the most part been neglected.[1] I believe the major reason for this neglect is Aristotle's reputation as
an unfair judge of Plato. For example, according to Susemihl and Hicks (1894),
Aristotle's criticisms of the *Republic*, though often successful, contain "mis-
apprehensions in particulars, some of which are very serious" (21, 32-33). One
such "misapprehension" is supposed to occur in the first criticism, which concerns the unity of the city (*polis*).

> The main defects of this criticism are at once apparent; Zeller . . . has
> rightly traced them to an excessive striving after logical clearness; a
> tendency to reduce the Platonic utterances to a number of precise dogmatic
> propositions and to test the independent validity of each empirically,
> without regard to its inner connexion with the whole system of idealism.
> Hence it comes about that the spirit of the Platonic teaching is hardly ever
> adequately appreciated, while now and then there is a captious, almost
> pedantic, disposition to get at external results and to fasten on details with
> but little insight into their relative importance. . . . This is the sober fact,
> and serves to account for the piquant charges of injustice, sophistry, and
> mala fides sometimes brought against Aristotle (215).[2]

1

More recently, Annas (1981, 188) has written that these criticisms are "often surprisingly crass and literal-minded, much below Aristotle's best."[3] This is a typical verdict on *Pol.* II 1-5, and it has led many scholars to dismiss these chapters as unimportant.[4]

I do not mean to suggest that everyone who has passed judgment on these chapters has condemned them. Some have taken them seriously and have been quite sympathetic, while others have lavished such praise on them that they seem to accept what Bornemann (1923, 71) called "das Dogma von der wissenschaftlichen Unfehlbarkeit des großen Stagiriten." Benardete (1989, 117), for instance, claims that "Aristotle's objections to the communism of women and children are so obvious that it is hardly necessary to prove that Socrates was as aware of them." (Cf. Bloom [1968, 386].) But this is fantastic. Aristotle's criticisms are not obviously true; in fact, it is not even obvious in every case what exactly he is trying to say. He is often brief, obscure, and incomplete. This is perhaps the strongest criticism that can be leveled against *Pol.* II 1-5.[5]

In this essay I shall attempt to bring to light what Aristotle is saying in criticizing the best city of the *Republic*. To this end I shall present a *philosophical* commentary on *Pol.* II 1-5. By "philosophical commentary" I mean that although it will sometimes be necessary to discuss purely historical or philological matters, my main concern will always be the philosophical content of the passages on which I am commenting. I shall not cover everything in these chapters, only those parts that are arguably the most important philosophically. And because so many of these criticisms are brief, obscure, and/or incomplete, I shall also be relying a great deal on the rest of the corpus (and especially on the rest of the *Politics*) in coming to grips with Aristotle's arguments.

The most unfortunate result of the neglect of these chapters is, of course, a failure to discover what they have to tell us about Aristotle's political philosophy. I hope to show that in *Pol.* II 1-5 Aristotle is presenting his views on what turns out to be an extremely fundamental issue: the unity of the city. Almost all of Aristotle's criticisms of the *Republic*, in varying degrees, center on this, and it was for him (no less than it was for Plato) a very important issue. Moreover, only by discovering Aristotle's views on the proper unity of the city can we adequately discover his views on the relationship between the individual and the city. This will in turn aid us in better understanding Aristotle's political thought generally.

Nicomachean Ethics X 9 (1181b12-22): An Outline for Political Science

At the end of the *Nicomachean Ethics*, Aristotle announces his plans for political science:

Since our predecessors have left the subject of legislation unexamined, it is perhaps best to investigate it ourselves instead, and to investigate constitutions in general, in order to complete the philosophy of human affairs as far as we are able.[6] [1] So first, if anything has been said well in part by our predecessors, let us go through it. [2] Then from the collected constitutions, let us study what sorts of things preserve and destroy cities and the particular types of constitution, and by what causes some are well governed and others the opposite. [3] For when we have studied these things, we will perhaps be more likely to see what sort of constitution is best, how each should be ordered, and what laws and habits it should use (1181b12-22).

In *Pol.* II, Aristotle examines the views of several of his predecessors (which corresponds to [1] above);[7] and he obviously thinks such an examination contributes to [3]: discovering the best constitution. But how? More specifically, what role does the criticism of Plato's *Republic* play in this broader goal? To answer these questions, we shall have to look at *Pol.* II 1 and the beginning of *Pol.* II 2, where Aristotle tells us how and why he critically examines the *Republic*.

Politics II 1 (1260b27-36): The Purpose of *Politics* II

In *Pol.* I 1 we learn that every city is a kind of community, and that the city is in fact the most authoritative and all-embracing community. In the rest of book I there is a discussion of the other types of community that the city embraces—the different parts of the city. The community of male and female, and the community of master and slave go to make up another community, the household. Households form the village community, and many villages make up a city, the political community.

At the end of book I, Aristotle says "let us first investigate the views that have been put forward concerning the best constitution" (1260b23-24). He begins book II as follows:

Since we intend to study political community—that which is the most excellent of all to those capable of living to the highest degree according to what one would pray for (*kat' euchên*)—we should also investigate other constitutions, both those that some of the cities that are said to have good laws use, and any others that are [only] spoken about by others [i.e., exist in speech alone] and are considered to be fine, so that what is correct and useful will be seen (1260b27-33).[8]

Aristotle's ultimate aim is to study the best political community—the best city. His purpose is accomplished in the last two books of the *Politics*, where he presents his own view of the best city. The purpose of book II is to contribute to this broader goal. In book II, Aristotle examines the constitutions that are considered best in order to discover what is correct and useful in them (and to avoid and expose what is not).[9] This will aid him in his attempt to discover what the best constitution is. (In keeping with this aim, I shall often, in the chapters that follow, go beyond Aristotle's criticisms of the *Republic* and show what they tell us about his own views of what is best.)

The "other constitutions" (i.e., other than his own) that Aristotle investigates in *Pol.* II can be divided into two categories:

1. Theoretical "best" constitutions (constitutions that exist only in speech and are held to be fine), found in or advocated by:
   i. Plato's *Republic* (*Pol.* II 1-5)
   ii. Plato's *Laws* (*Pol.* II 6)
   iii. Phaleas of Chalcedon (*Pol.* II 7)
   iv. Hippodamus of Miletus (*Pol.* II 8).
2. Actual "best" constitutions ("those that some of the cities that are said to have good laws use"[10]):
   i. Lakedaemonian (*Pol.* II 9)
   ii. Cretan (*Pol.* II 10)
   iii. Carthaginian (*Pol.* II 11).[11]

But why does Aristotle intend to study that political community which is the most excellent of all "to those capable of living to the highest degree according to what one would pray for"? Why does he not just say he intends to study the best political community or constitution? The answer can in part be found in *Pol.* II 6, where he criticizes a particular feature of the constitution in Plato's *Laws*. There he says that "certainly, what one assumes should be according to what one would pray for, but surely nothing should be impossible" (1265a17-18). What one would pray for is the wider category, including both possible and impossible things. Aristotle is concerned with the best constitution without qualification, given no impediments—i.e., the best constitution possible to the best men under the best circumstances. (See *Pol.* 1325b32-39.)

Aristotle felt the need to stress that the best political community must in some sense be possible. Thus he probably thought many of those who put forward views on the best constitution dealt in impossibilities. As we have seen, he criticized Plato for making what one would pray for impossible, and this does seem to be a fair criticism. (See *Rep.* 450d, 456b-c, 499c, 540d, and *Laws* 736d. But cf. *Laws* 742e.) One of his objections to those who make the best—what one would pray for—impossible, is that to the extent that their views are impossible, they are neither correct nor useful. (See *Pol.* 1288b35-37).[12]

Politics II 1 (1260b36-61a9):
How Much Should Citizens Share in Common?

Aristotle says that we must make the "natural beginning," and that is determining how much citizens should share in common (*Pol.* 1260b37-39). The natural beginning of the study of political community (*koinônia*) is answering the question: Should the citizens have in common (*koinônein*) everything or nothing or some but not all things? A natural place to begin an inquiry into political community is to investigate the extent of the community. Answering this question becomes the major motivation behind his criticism of Plato's *Republic*.

How much *should* citizens share in common? There are only three possibilities: Nothing, everything, and some things but not others. Aristotle wants to proceed by eliminating two of these. The one that remains will be correct. First, he says that "clearly, to have nothing in common is impossible, for the constitution is a community, and it is first necessary to have a location in common. There is [one] location to one city, and the citizens are companions (*koinônioi*) in the one city" (*Pol.* 1260b39-61a1). One possible answer was easy to rule out. But instead of trying to eliminate one of the two remaining answers on the grounds of impossibility, he proceeds with the following question: "Is it better for the city that is going to be managed finely to have everything in common, or is it better to have some things in common but not others?" (*Pol.* 1261a2-4). Aristotle proceeds in this way because he believes that "it is possible for citizens to have in common between themselves children, women, and possessions, as in Plato's *Republic*; for there Socrates asserts that children, women, and possessions should be common (*koina*)" (*Pol.* 1261a4-8). So Aristotle holds that it is at least *possible* for citizens to have everything in common.[13] (He cannot rule this out on the grounds of impossibility.) Aristotle may be using a loose sense of "possible" here, such that it is "possible" for citizens to have everything in common because it has come to be in writing (and therefore should be considered). Or, despite his criticism that Plato sometimes aims at what is impossible, Aristotle might find in the best constitution of Plato's *Republic* much (or at least something) that is really possible. And this may have been confirmed by stories of people actually having everything, or almost everything, in common.[14]

Aristotle has shown that it is impossible for citizens to have nothing in common and that it is in some sense possible for them to have everything in common. And of course, it is possible to have some things in common, but not others, because that "is the way it is now" (*Pol.* 1261a8). It remains to determine whether it is better to have everything in common or not, and this Aristotle attempts through his criticism of Plato's *Republic*.

It is worth noting that if we keep in mind that the purpose of *Pol.* II 1-5 is primarily to determine what citizens ought to share in common, we should not be puzzled by the fact that there is so much in the *Republic* that Aristotle does *not* discuss and/or criticize in these chapters. His attack on the *Republic* has a narrow focus. (See Stalley [1991, 184-86] and Saunders [1995, 106].)

Politics II 2 (1261a10-16): End and Means

Aristotle says "there are many other difficulties[15] in women being common (*koinas*) to all (*pantôn*)"[16] (*Pol.* 1261a10-11), but he goes on to name only two of them. It is best to first look at the end of this passage—Socrates' assumption—before these two difficulties because it is involved in both of them. According to Aristotle, the assumption of Socrates in the *Republic* is that "the city being entirely one, to the highest degree, is best" (taking *pasan* with *mian*, not *polin*) (*Pol.* 1261a15-16). There are no real problems here: this is an accurate description of what Socrates says in the *Republic*. (See 423d, 462a-e, and cf. *Laws* 739c-d.) According to Socrates, the highest degree of unity in the city is the greatest good. This is the standard by which he judges the community of women, children, and property, and it is the goal at which he aims.

Aristotle states that one difficulty with Socrates' communism is that "the reason for which Socrates asserts that laws should be made in this way clearly does not follow from his arguments" (1261a11-12). At *Rep.* 462a-e we see that the reason laws are made in this way—i.e., communistically—is that the Socratic assumption mentioned above is thought best. Thus, according to Aristotle, Plato's Socrates has not made a case for the standard and aim (or end) of the best city. It is his central task in *Pol.* II 2 to attack this aim. There he will attempt to demonstrate why the highest degree of unity in a city is not best.

A second difficulty is that "with regard to the end which [Socrates] asserts should belong to the city, as it was stated [in the *Republic*] it is impossible, but how one should interpret this is nowhere determined"[17] (*Pol.* 1261a13-14). The end, of course, is the highest degree of unity. So what Aristotle is saying is that even if the highest degree of unity were the correct aim of the city (and it is not), it is impossible to reach it by means of the communism of women, children, and property found in the *Republic*. (See *Pol.* 1331b26-34.) This he attempts to demonstrate in *Pol.* II 3-5.[18]

How Aristotle Reads the *Republic*

With rare exceptions, Aristotle refers to the communism of the *Republic* as Socrates' scheme (the Socrates of the *Republic*, of course).[19] For those (e.g. Straussians) who maintain that the best city of the *Republic* somehow negatively implies Plato's own views, Aristotle's practice might seem to support their position. But as Stalley (1991, 183n5) points out: "This need not mean that Aristotle intends to distance Plato from the 'Socrates' he criticizes. In the concluding section of book II he attributes some of the main proposals in the *Republic* to Plato (12.1274b9-11)."[20] But since my concern is what Aristotle's criticisms reveal about his own political philosophy, not how to read a Platonic dialogue, I can sidestep this issue.[21]

Moving to a more controversial point, in criticizing the *Republic*, Aristotle seems to operate under the assumption that Plato's communism applies in some form to all citizens, not simply to the ruling class. This may be the major reason behind his reputation as an unfair and unsympathetic reader of the *Republic*. He would argue, however, that he has some justification in doing so. In *Pol.* II 5, he writes:

> what the scheme of the whole constitution will be for those sharing in it, Socrates has not said, nor is it easy to say. And yet the multitude of the city [i.e., all the citizens] turns out to be nearly [the same as] the multitude of the other citizens [i.e., the iron and bronze citizens], concerning whom nothing has been determined, whether among the farmers as well possessions should be common or private to each individual, and further, whether women and children should be private or common (1264a11-17).

Scholars are nearly unanimous in rejecting this reading of the *Republic*. I think Aristotle is right, however, and defend his position in the appendix. If I am correct, then an important part of the case against Aristotle as an unfair critic of Plato has been destroyed.

But if Plato is unclear, why does Aristotle operate under the assumption that the communism of the *Republic* applies to all citizens? The reason may be the narrow, focused aims of these criticisms: to discover what or how much citizens should share in common and to contribute to an understanding of the best constitution. And if this assumption is *not* correct, Aristotle argues, and the lifestyle of the rulers is radically different from that of the workers, then this will itself cause problems. For example, there would be two cities instead of one, with the guardians in the role of something like a garrison. (See *Pol.* 1264a17-32.) So, Aristotle would claim he is not distorting Plato unfairly to serve his purpose. Instead, he is taking one plausible reading of the *Republic* and criticizing it to serve his purpose.

Summary

Aristotle has two related aims in criticizing Plato's *Republic*. First, he wants to know what citizens should possess in common—that is why he undertook this investigation in the first place. Second, communistic ideas were in the air—a part of intellectual debate (perhaps most of all in the Academy)—and Aristotle wanted to refute them. These aims were best served through a critical examination of the best city of the *Republic*.[22]

Aristotle carries off this critical examination by first attacking the *aim* of Platonic communism (in *Pol.* II 2). I discuss these criticisms in chapters 2 and 3. He then attacks the communism of women, children, and property as *means* to the aim of Platonic communism (in *Pol.* II 3-5). I discuss these arguments in chapters 4 and 5.

Notes

1. Some of the works dealing directly with *Pol.* II 1-5 are: Bornemann (1923), Nussbaum (1980), Saxonhouse (1982), Dobbs (1985), Simpson (1991), and Stalley (1991). Bornemann (1923, 71-72) mentions much of the pre-twentieth-century literature.

2. Although this work was not a cooperative effort, but a revision and translation by Hicks of an earlier work by Susemihl, for simplicity's sake I shall always refer to "Susemihl and Hicks" regardless of who is responsible for the particular passage cited.

3. Other negative opinions on these chapters include: Bornemann (1923), Mulgan (1977, 29, 39), and Saunders (1992, 103, 106-7, 113). Dobbs (1985, 30n3) and Simpson (1991, 99n1) provide more examples of negative evaluations of Aristotle's criticisms of the *Republic*.

This harsh view of Aristotle fits with his reputation as a historian and critic of earlier philosophers. Cherniss (1964, ix) writes that "it has long been vaguely recognized that Aristotle was capable of setting down something other than the objective truth when he had occasion to write about his predecessors." Aristotle, Cherniss maintains, saw in his predecessors "'stammering' attempts to express his own system," and by interpreting them in the way he wanted—in the way that served his purposes—he could reintegrate these half-true views into his own correct position. This naturally, it is claimed, led to the distortion of his predecessors' theories (1964, 348, 404). In these passages Cherniss is specifically discussing Aristotle's treatment of the pre-Socratics, but he clearly thinks these claims apply to Aristotle's treatment of Plato as well (even to Aristotle's criticisms of Plato's political philosophy). (See Cherniss [1944, ix, xi, xx].)

4. On the whole, I believe this verdict is incorrect. Although it is not primarily my purpose to examine whether or to what extent Aristotle was fair to Plato, I believe that we shall see (in passing) that in most cases Aristotle's criticisms of the *Republic* are well founded (or at least not obviously incorrect, as many scholars seem to think).

5. Stalley (1991, 186) writes that *Pol.* II "does not look like a finished work. If what we have is, in effect, a set of notes, it is not surprising that they should appear incomplete and unbalanced."

6. Aristotle writes that "our predecessors have left the subject of legislation unexamined." Michael of Ephesus correctly comments:

> Since, [Aristotle] asserts, our predecessors have left off speaking about laws and constitutions (clearly the best [constitutions]), we ourselves must investigate these things. And he does not mean that none of those before him set up laws and proposed constitutions (for many, whom he examines in the *Politics*, became lawgivers, and wrote political treatises, even Plato himself); what he means is that since none of those before us investigated these things accurately, and they all were ignorant of the nature of the true and best constitutions, let us ourselves attempt to say what is better (*In Ethica Nicomachea*, CAG XX 619).

7. Aristotle often begins an inquiry by investigating the views of his predecessors. See *DA* I, *Met*. I, *Phys*. I, etc.

8. Newman (1887, 2:xxi-xxii, 225-27) has argued that the end of book I and the opening of book II are inconsistent because the first book claims that the opinions put forth on the best constitutions must be discussed next, whereas the second book covers more than just these opinions. But this hardly counts against Aristotle or the consistency of the two books. Aristotle begins with opinions concerning the best constitutions and from there naturally moves on to a discussion of the actual constitutions that are held to be best. See Saunders (1995, 104).

9. Stalley (1991, 183) rightly points out that at least in the case of Plato, Aristotle focuses on the negative aim: pointing out what is *not* good or useful.

10 See Xenophon, *Mem*. IV 4.15 (on Sparta); Plato, *Crito* 52e (on Crete and Sparta); Plato[?], *Minos* 320b (on Crete and Sparta); and Polybius VI 43 (on Sparta, Crete, and Carthage).

11. *Pol*. II 12, the final chapter of book II, is a brief and unusual discussion of some famous lawgivers. On the issue of its authenticity, see Keaney (1981).

12. Aristotle goes on to say that another (albeit lesser) reason for the investigation of these other constitutions is that when, in the end, he seeks something other than these constitutions (and this is basically what he does in *Pol*. III-VIII) he will not be thought to be setting up some best constitution of his own simply to appear clever; instead he will be thought (correctly) to be undertaking the investigation (and criticism) of these other constitutions because those that now exist are not good (and the proposals for their improvement are inadequate) and thus need to be corrected (*Pol*. 1260b33-36).

13. By "everything" Aristotle means "women, children, and property." As Newman (1887, 2:229) points out, some things cannot be shared. (See *Rep*. 464d.)

14. At the beginning of *Pol*. II 7, Aristotle says that "no one else [besides Plato] has been innovative concerning the community of women and children . . ." (1266a34-35). However, some others, it seems, have advocated a community of property, or something similar. Of these, "Phaleas of Chalcedon was the first . . . , for he said it is necessary for the possessions of the citizens to be equal" (1266a39-40). (Susemihl and Hicks [1894, 261-62] state that Phaleas must have "come forward with his political scheme before Plato published either of his." Newman [1887, 2:283] suggests Phaleas was an older contemporary of Plato.) In the last chapter of book II, Aristotle says that "Peculiar to

Phaleas is the leveling of property, and to Plato, the community of women, children, and property . . ." (1274b9-11). Does this mean that no one advocated, discussed, or knew of the communism of property, women, and children before Plato and Phaleas? Clearly not. Aristotle himself writes that some Libyans had women in common (*Pol.* 1262a19-21), thus showing that others knew of, and even practiced, the community of women. (For some historical accounts of communal or communistic peoples whom Plato and Aristotle may have been aware of, see: Herodotus I 216, IV 104, 172, 180; Xanthas fr. 31 [Jacoby]; Theopompus fr. 204 [Jacoby]; and Ephors fr. 42 [Jacoby].) Ussher (1973, xix) says that Aristotle of course knew of Aristophanes' *Ecclesiazusae* and that in the above-cited passages from the *Politics*, Aristotle is only "speaking of those who have put forward opinions *peri politeias*," and a comedy would not qualify. (For the communistic scheme parodied in the *Ecclesiazusae* [first performed in 393 or 392] see lines 571-727. Cf. Euripides fr. 402 and fr. 653 [Nauck] for another playwright who dealt with some of these issues.) Thus, we can conclude that Aristotle did not believe that the communism of property, women, and children (or any combination of the three) first appeared in the works of Plato and Phaleas. That these ideas did not originate with Plato, however, does not imply that they were ordinary or commonplace during his lifetime (see *Rep.* 449c and *Tim.* 18c). But they were certainly in the air when Plato wrote the *Republic* and Aristotle criticized it.

I should like to offer the following educated guess as to how the ideas with which I am concerned in this essay may have (at least in part) become part of the intellectual atmosphere: Perhaps some thinkers, pessimistic about how things were going in Greek cities during certain periods, saw a solution to their problems in the (often overly optimistic) reports of communal bliss coming from some travelers and historians. (Cf. Diodorus Siculus II 55-60.) There are modern parallels: reports from the South Pacific in the eighteenth century (picked up by Rousseau, for instance); the views of twentieth century Marxist anthropologists on primitive societies. For a good example of a romanticized (and inaccurate) picture of tribal life, see Herman Melville's *Typee* (1846), especially chapter 17. McInnes (1972) writes: "Sound information played no role in the many communist projects. Their authors were content with tenuous legends (the Atlantis of Plato's Critias or the Sparta of Plutarch's Lycurgus) or with scraps of misinformation ("noble savages" in the New World)." However, not all of the reports the Greeks received were positive (e.g., Xenophon, *Anabasis* V 4, 33-34, and Apollonius Rhodius III 1023-25).

Plato and Aristotle also knew about Sparta, which may have been characterized by some communistic institutions. See: Xenophon *LC* VII 1-3; Polybius VI 45, 48, XII 6; and Plutarch, *Lycurgus* VIII 1-4, IX 1-3, XIII 5, XV 7-14, XVI 1, XVII 1, XXIV 1, XXV 3, 5.

15. "Other" here means "other than the two difficulties that will be mentioned shortly." Aristotle may have in mind the assorted criticisms found at the end of *Pol.* II 4 (1262b24-36) and *Pol.* II 5 (1264a1-b25). Stalley (1991, 197) writes: "These arguments have little, if any, bearing on the concept of community which has dominated Aristotle's discussion up to this point. In so far as they have any common theme it is that Plato has not thought through the practical implications of his proposals."

16. At the end of *Pol.* II 1, Aristotle mentioned children, women, and property, whereas here he only mentions women. This is probably just an oversight—or shorthand for "women, children, and property"—since the remainder of *Pol.* II 2 deals with issues pertaining to the community of all three.

Susemihl and Hicks (1894, 215) state that *pantôn* and *koinas* are "unintentional misrepresentations" of what Plato said, i.e., it was unfair of Aristotle to say that Plato advocated that women be common to all. "The 'marriage laws' in question affect only Plato's Guardians, and do not establish community of wives at all, in the strictly literal and unfavourable sense of the term. . . ." In response I should like to make four points: (1) Aristotle employs the same language as Plato, where, at *Rep.* 457c-d, Socrates uses *pantôn* and *koinas*. (2) Although it is obvious from the context of Plato's discussion at 457c-d that he is referring to the community of women or wives among the guardians, this is not always the case in the *Republic*, and Aristotle makes it clear at *Pol.* 1264a11-b6 that he (Aristotle) thinks (or proceeds as if) the question of whether the communism of women, children, and property applies to all classes or to the guardian class alone has not been settled. (See the appendix.) (3) It may be that Aristotle thinks it is improper for "all" to have women in common, whether "all" refers to all citizens or all guardians. (4) By "strictly literal and unfavourable," Susemihl and Hicks mean a promiscuous sharing of women in common. They remark that Aristotle does not criticize the community of women in the *Republic* on the grounds of license, but still somehow they think the way he expresses himself here (unintentionally) suggests that the community of women in the *Republic* is some kind of orgy. But the misunderstanding is Susemihl and Hicks's, not Aristotle's. He finds the community of women unfavorable, but he does not regard promiscuity as the only sense in which such a community could be unfavorable. (There will, of course, be more discussion on the ways the community of women is unfavorable according to Aristotle.)

17. The most difficult part of this passage philologically is *hôs eirêtai nun*. This is most naturally translated "as has just been said" (see Lord's translation). But the only things that have just been said in this regard are that Socrates' view that the highest degree of unity in the city is best does not follow from his arguments, and (in the previous chapter) that it is possible (in a sense) to have women, children, and property in common. But neither of these fits the more natural translation. It is better to translate in the way I have above: "as it was stated," which is at least grammatically possible. *Nun* can often mean "as it is," "as the case stands"; and it seems that in certain contexts, it can mean roughly "in the case under discussion," "in the case supposed." See Liddell, Scott, and Jones, s.v., and Smyth (1956, sec. 2924). (Cf. *Pol.* 1261b24.) Susemihl and Hicks (1894, 216) claim that in our passage *nun* means "in the case supposed." Also see Newman (1887, 2:229). At *Pol.* 1268a34, *nun* seems to mean "as the case stands" with "according to Hippodamus's scheme" implied. In the present case I leave the *nun* untranslated, translating *hôs eirêtai* "as was stated," with the *nun* implying "in the *Republic*."

18. For an alternative interpretation of the "plan" of *Pol.* II 2-5, see Simpson (1991, 100-3).

19. Aristotle mentions Plato's name only once in *Pol.* II 1-5, in referring to Plato's *Republic* (1261a6; see also 1266b5, 1274b9). For the rest he refers to Socrates: See 1261a12, 1261a16, 1261b19, 1261b21, 1262b6, 1262b9, 1263b30, 1264a12, 1264a29, 1264b7, 1264b29, 1264b37.

20. The authenticity of this passage from *Pol.* II 12 has often been denied or doubted (see, for example, Susemihl and Hicks [1894, 320] and Newman [1887, 2:382-83]), but there are reasons for thinking its inclusion in the chapter is not improper. (See Keaney [1981, 99].)

21. Throughout this book, I shall for the most part speak of "Plato," "Plato's communism," etc.

22. For convenience sake, I shall often use "Kallipolis" to refer to the best city of the *Republic*. (See *Rep.* 527d.)

Chapter Two

The Unity of the City

They do not recognize that the most wonderful thing about political concord is that it makes unity out of plurality and similarity out of dissimilarity.
Pseudo-Aristotle, *De Mundo* 396b4-6

And discord follow upon unison,
And all things at one common level lie.
W. B. Yeats, "These Are the Clouds"

Politics II 2 (1261a16-b6):
The First Criticism of the Aim of Communism

Aristotle begins his criticism of the *Republic* with an attack on the *aim* of Plato's best city, Kallipolis: the highest degree of unity. He says that it is clear that as the city

> advances and becomes more of a unity (*mia*), it will not even be a city. For the city is, with regard to its nature, some multitude (*plêthos ti*), and becoming more of a unity, it will be a household rather than a city, and a human being rather than a household. For we would say that the household is more of a unity than the city, and the individual more than the household. So even if someone were able to do this, he ought not do it; for this would destroy the city (*Pol.* 1261a16-22; cf. 1263b29-35).

Aristotle mentions two kinds of unity that are too much unity for the city. These will act as upper limits. Why two? (After all, you only need one to set a limit.) He does so simply because Plato, at different times, attributes both kinds of unity to Kallipolis.[1]

Obviously, part of what is involved here is the fact that the city is a multitude (and at *Pol.* 1261a22-b9 Aristotle gives us some idea of what he has in mind). But there must be more to his criticism than this, for even Kallipolis has many different parts. It turns out that his criticism also involves the diversity of parts and how these parts are connected in a city, household, and individual, and the different ends that cities, households, and individuals have. For only a change in these respects could destroy a city (assuming, of course, that cities, households, and individuals are more than just quantitatively different, which is also an issue). These issues are central, and I shall return to them in this chapter after a discussion of *Pol.* 1261a22-31.

Not only is a city different in composition and aim from a household and individual, it is also different from an alliance (*summachia*) and an Arkadia-like nation (or race, *ethnos*). (Because the unity of the alliance and of the Arkadian type of nation are basically the same, I shall consider only the alliance.[2]) In mentioning the difference between a city and an alliance, Aristotle sets a lower limit on the kind of unity a city should have, and he gives us some idea of just what kind of multitude a city is. "Not only is the city made up of a number of human beings, but also of a number of human beings differing in kind (*eidei*). For a city does not come to be out of similar people" (*Pol.* 1261a22-24; cf. 1277a5-11). The alliance illustrates this point. "A city and an alliance are different. For the usefulness of an alliance is in its numbers, even if its parts are the same in kind, since the alliance exists by nature for the sake of assistance, just as if an [additional] weight were to draw down the scales more" (*Pol.* 1261a24-27). An alliance is not made up of parts that are different in kind. It is "an aggregate of homogeneous members. The separate autonomous states, the Lacedaemonians and their allies, for example, are homogeneous" (Susemihl and Hicks [1894, 216-17]). In addition, the aim of an alliance is basically military usefulness. Thus, the more members added to an alliance, the better or stronger it becomes. But a city does not become greater with an increase in the number of its parts. (See *Pol.* 1326a8-25.) What distinguishes a city is not so much the number of its parts, but the types of parts, their connection, and the city's function and end as a whole.

Having contrasted the city with the alliance, Aristotle reiterates a point he made before: "those out of which a unity should come to be differ in kind." He says that we can conclude from this that "reciprocal equality (*to ison to antipeponthos*) preserves (*sôizei*) cities, as was said earlier in the *Ethics*" (*Pol.* 1261a29-31). The force of this conclusion is not that something preserves cities, but just what that something is. And further, not that it is a type of equality or justice, but precisely what type of justice and equality. But what is reciprocal equality, and how does it preserve cities? We must go to "the *Ethics*" to find out. Such an investigation will reveal a lot about what the unity of the city is, for it will tell us much about how the city is held together. But since I am now

concerned not so much with the unity of the city as I am with the limits to that
unity, I shall postpone this investigation until we are ready to discuss the unity
of the city as such.

So far we know what the limits to the unity of the city are (i.e., the kinds of
unity the city can *not* possess). I should next like to examine Aristotle's views
on unity *per se*, before treating separately the four kinds of unity that concern
us.

Part, Whole, and Unity

In *Met.* V 6, Aristotle distinguishes two senses in which things are called
"one" or "a unity": "now most things are called one (*hen*) from doing or possessing or being affected by or being related to some other thing that is one, but
the things that are called one in the primary way are those whose substance is
one" (1016b6-9; see also 1015b36-1016a18). The first sense of "one" or "unity"
is derivative, whereas the other is the primary sense and applies to substances
(e.g., animals). This distinction between the two senses of "unity" is similar in
some important respects to the distinction Aristotle makes between two senses
of "whole."

Aristotle begins *Met.* VII 16 with the following:

> It is evident that even of the things that are thought to be substances, most
> are [only] potentialities (*dunameis*): the parts of animals (for none of them,
> having been separated, is [the part of an animal], and when they are sepa-
> rated, then all of them exist [merely] as matter) and earth and fire and air;
> for none of them is one (*hen*), but they are like a heap, until they are con-
> cocted and some one thing comes to be out of them. . . . All [the parts] will
> exist [only] potentially (*dunamei*) when they are one and continuous by na-
> ture (1040b5-15).

Ross (1924, 2:218) states that *dunameis* here refers to those things "capable of
contributing to the life of the whole . . . ," and this is correct. Parts of animals
are potentialities or capabilities—they exist only when and insofar as they can
perform a function that contributes to the well-being of the whole animal. Otherwise they are (or are part of) a heap. "What every thing is," Aristotle writes
in the *Meteorology*, "is determined by its function. Each thing truly is [what it
is] when it is able to perform its own function, e.g., the eye when it can see"
(390a10-11). And in the case of the parts of living organisms, the function—
and hence what it is—is inextricably bound to the whole organism. This is why
a part that has been separated from a living organism (or a part of a corpse) is a
part in name only. (See *Meteor.* 389b30-390a1 and 390a12-13; *PA* 640b29-
641a21; *DA* 412b18-24; *GA* 734b25-28, 735a8.) In such cases they are not even

dunameis. (The *Met.* VII 16 sense of *dunamis* is operative in the biology. See, for instance, *PA* 640b17-24, 646b11-28.)

Clearly, the same notion of *dunamis* is employed in the following important passage from Aristotle's discussion of "wholes" in *Met.* V 26: "What is continuous and limited [is a whole] when it is some one thing made up of several [parts], especially when these constituents of it are potential (*dunamei*), but if not, when they are actual (*energeia*). Of these things themselves, that which is so by nature is more [a whole] than what is artificially" (1023b32-35). The potential constituents Aristotle refers to are the same parts of animals that exist only "potentially," i.e., for the sake of the whole organism, i.e., to the extent that they perform a function that supports the life and well-being of the organism. Actual constituents form "lesser" unities (and "lesser" wholes) because they could be separated from the whole and still exist and function in their characteristic way. (E.g., the beam that forms part of a house can be, say, a lintel *or* a threshold. See *Met.* 1042b19-20.) And they cannot all be held together internally. They are, in a sense, themselves wholes. But the potential constituents, which go to make up natural unities, are by their very nature parts of a whole and thus form a whole whose unity is much tighter. (All of this is in fact implied in Aristotle's crucial claim that substances cannot be composed out of substances [*Met.* 1039a3-4, 1041a4-5].)

Substances are greater unities and greater wholes than nonsubstances.[3] And we should expect the parts of substances and nonsubstances to differ accordingly, as well as their unity. Thus, whereas the unity of the individual (which is the unity of a substance) is a primary sort of unity, the unities of households, cities, and alliances are not. (More on this distinction after the discussion of the unity of substances.)

The Unity of a Substance

In the *Republic*, Plato holds that the unity of the best city should be the unity of the individual human being (462a-e; cf. *Laws* 739c-d). Thus Plato thinks that the unity of (what Aristotle calls) substance is a proper standard by which to judge the unity of the city. It is a degree of unity the city should aim for. Aristotle denies this when he writes that if the city becomes too much of a unity, it becomes a human being and will no longer be a city (*Pol.* 1261a18-20). In order to fully understand Aristotle's position, it is necessary to examine what the unity of the individual (i.e., the unity of substance) is according to Aristotle.

First, how are the parts of a substance (i.e., the parts of an animal) held together to form one natural whole? (1) Each part is connected physically with the organism, and cannot be separated and remain a part of that organism.[4] (2)

The parts exist solely for the organism of which they are a part; they are defined by the function they perform for that organism. (3) These parts do not (and cannot) in any real sense exist independently or in their own right: They exist only "potentially" (or as potentials), i.e., they are capacities (*dunameis*) belonging to the entity of which they are parts; they are not themselves entities.[5]

The city must have less unity than this. Now obviously, the parts of the city are not physically continuous, and thus its unity is qualitatively different from the unity of an individual. But the parts of the household are not continuous, and it has less unity than a substance, yet more than a city. This implies that the city lacks the unity of a substance for reasons other than physical continuity alone. Thus the city should not be characterized by points 2 and 3 either (or not to the same degree).

The unity of substance serves as an upper limit in our attempt to discover the unity of the city. As we have seen, the parts of communities (and thus the parts of cities) cannot be continuous (which involves their being physically connected). Individuals are separable from a city in a way parts of animals are not. Sever a leg from a horse and it begins to decay almost immediately. Not so with individuals when "severed" from their city. If a person leaves his city, he does not die. A person can leave one city and go to live in another. A city might be destroyed, without any of its citizens being destroyed (cf. *Top.* 150a33-36).[6] Related to this is the fact that the same group of people can become a different city (*Pol.* 1276b4-8).[7] Aristotle also suggests in *Pol.* VII 2-3 that some individuals are capable of living a life separated, in a sense, from the activities of the city, and not related to or involving others: the philosopher (1324a14-17, 1324a25-32, 1325b16-21; cf. 1267a10-12).[8] There is no counterpart to this among the parts of animals.

But more importantly, Aristotle's distinction between the unity of the city and the unity of substance shows that the parts of a city: (1) most likely should not exist solely for the sake of the city of which they are parts; and (2) are most likely independent in some nontrivial way. Free men are not *of* some other human being(s)—i.e., they do not belong to another. Aristotle's discussion of slavery supports this. In *Pol.* I 4, he writes:

> The possession is spoken of just as the part (*morion*) is. For the part is not only a part of another, but also is of another (*allou*) [i.e., belongs to another] wholly (*holôs*, or without qualification, *haplôs*).[9] Similarly with a possession. Thus, the master is only master of the slave, but does not belong to him, while the slave is not only a slave of the master, but also belongs to him wholly. . . . One who does not belong to himself by nature (*mê hauto phusei*), but though a human being belongs to another, this man is by nature a slave (1254a8-15).[10]

In *Met.* I he says that "the man is free who is [or exists] for the sake of himself (*hautou heneka*) and not [for the sake] of another" (982b25-26).[11]

But then what is Aristotle saying at *Pol.* I 2, where he wrote the following?

> The man who is without a city (*apolis*) through nature and not through chance is either low or greater than a man, just like the one denounced by Homer: "clanless, lawless, heartless". . . . In addition, the city is prior by nature to the household and to each of us, since it is necessary for the whole to be prior to the part. For if the whole [body] is destroyed, there will be no foot or hand, unless homonymously, just as if someone were to say the stone [hand is a hand]; for [a hand] when destroyed will be such [i.e., no better than a stone hand], but everything is defined by its function [or activity, *ergôi*] and its *dunamei*. . . . So, that the city is both by nature and prior to each [individual] is clear. For if the individual having been separated is not self-sufficient, he will be in a state similar to the other parts in relation to the whole, but he who is not able to be in a community or needs nothing through self-sufficiency is no part of a city, and so is either a beast or a god (1253a3-29).

This passage certainly makes it sound like the citizen is a part of the city in the strong sense of the term, but must we read the passage this way? I do not think so.

First, what does Aristotle mean when he says the city is prior by nature to the individual? There are several senses of priority (see *Met.* V 11; *Cat.* 12). But here, Aristotle clearly means the city is prior to the individual *by nature* (see *Pol.* 1253a25). He says things are called "prior according to nature and substance when it is possible for them to be without other things but not [these other things] without them" (*Met.* 1019a2-4; see *Cat.* 14a29-35). The city is prior to the individual in that the city can exist without any particular individual, but every individual human requires a city in order to exist (as a human).[12]

Second, what is meant by the analogy with the hand and the body in the *Pol.* I 2 passage? It is clear that the point Aristotle is trying to make is that both the hand when separated from the body and the individual when separated from the city are unable to perform their proper functions. A hand separated from a body cannot perform the functions of a hand; an individual when separated from the city cannot perform (all of) the functions proper to an individual (i.e., the characteristically human functions). The analogy is imperfect, but it still makes its point. (How the individual is unable to function when separated from the city will be discussed shortly.) What's important for our purposes is that we cannot automatically infer anything from this analogy about the metaphysical status of the city or its parts (e.g., that the city is an organism or quasi-organism).[13]

Finally, what happens to a man separated from the city? Greek literature provides us with two different examples that illustrate Aristotle's point fairly well. The first is Philoctetes, from Sophocles' play of the same name.[14] Philoctetes was well born (180). He wronged no one and lived equally (or justly) among equal (or just) men (683-84, *isos ôn isois anêr*). But because of a snakebite on his foot, which left him stinking and in great pain, he was abandoned on a desolate island, "without houses" (1-2, 6-7, 169-75). He still acts, but everything he does is aimed at keeping himself alive. This is made even more difficult because of his malady. He hunts, and lives in a hut. That is all (31-37, 162-68, 285-99). He says that he has become a savage (226; but cf. 1321), but still he longs to hear human (i.e., Greek) voices (225-31), or better, to go home (310-11, 468-506, 1213-17). It is true that his foot hinders him and makes his situation more difficult than it would have been if he had been marooned on an island with his health intact. Nevertheless, Philoctetes' plight provides us with an example of a man separated from a city. But is he not still a man? He claims that he is dead, a shadow of smoke, a phantom; desolate, without friends, without a city (*apolin*), he is a dead man among the living (946-47, 1018). But what would Aristotle say? Philoctetes is certainly unable to live a fully human life, and in that sense it might be true to say that he is not human. But if he were returned to a city (and his health were restored), he would be able to live fully and properly. He is, I think, what Aristotle would call someone separated from a city by chance and not by nature (*Pol.* 1253a3-4).

Let us now look at a being I think fulfills the requirements of being separated from the city by nature: the cyclops (described by Homer in *Odyssey* IX). The cyclopes are arrogant and wild cannibals, without law, custom, or real knowledge (106, 112-15, 189, 215, 287-92, 428). Each one is his own law, and cares nothing for others (except perhaps for his own wife and children). They possess no agriculture, trade, or shipbuilding, and no outside contact of any kind; they only tend their flocks and run households (of sorts) for their daily needs (107-11, 125-30, 183-86, 218-23). Aristotle in fact suggests that these households are examples of precity households (*Pol.* 1252b19-22). They are therefore separate from (and thus not a part of) a city. Now a cyclops (Polyphemos, for instance) is *by nature* separate from the city. It is not that he lacks the *opportunity* to exercise his capacities to the fullest and thus live a full human life; he lacks the *capacity* to live a full human life.[15] He is, much more than Philoctetes, not a human, or is a human in name only.[16]

We are now in a better position to know what exactly Aristotle means when he says the city is prior to the individual by nature. Humans are not *born* with the capacity to live full human lives. The opportunity to live such a life requires, for example, the cultivation of intellectual and moral virtues, which, Aristotle believes, can only take place in the context of a life lived in a political community.[17] In addition, a human being cannot live without the city because the city is required for the living of a full human life. Humans can perform their highest actions (e.g., virtuous actions, philosophy) only within the city (or after having lived in a city). This is why the city is prior to the individual.

This priority, however, does not imply that the individual lacks independence or is subordinated to the city in any full sense. That one can live his life fully only *in* the city does not mean that one must live a life wholly *for* the city. So although it is true to say of the leg of a dog, for instance, that it exists solely for the sake of the dog (or the life of the dog), it is not the case, according to Aristotle, that a human being exists solely for the sake of his city.[18]

The Unity of Communities

Households, cities, and alliances are communities (*koinôniai*), and no community is a unity in the primary sense, for each is a multitude (*plethos*) by nature,[19] and a multitude is the opposite of a unity. (See *Met.* 1004a10, 1054a20-22.) There are most likely two reasons for this opposition. First, as we have seen, every community is (ultimately) made up of substances and thus is not itself a substance. (See *Met.* 1039a3-4, 1041a4-5.) Second, continuity is essential to being a unity in the primary sense, and this requires that the parts that make up one thing are actually (i.e., physically) connected to some other part or parts of that thing at all times. But this of course is not found among the parts of communities. Thus a community can only be a unity in a secondary or derivative manner (as described in *Met.* V 6). He also says that the way a thing's parts are held together is the manner in which a thing is a unity (*Phys.* 227a15-16), and this would seem to apply to communities as well, at least in an analogous way. So the two questions that must be kept in mind when considering each of the communities that interest us are: (1) What is the one thing its parts are related to?[20] (2) What holds it together?[21]

The Unity of a Household

Aristotle tells us that the unity of a household is less than that of a substance, but greater than that of a city (*Pol.* 1261a18-20). Thus it too is an upper limit which the unity of the city must not surpass. To discover just what the unity of a household is, we must answer the two questions just posed with respect to the household.

How should we answer them?[22] First, the parts of the household go to make up one household by possessing one ruler. This gives the household a high degree of unity (for a community) because this one ruler has complete authority, and thereby gives the household one direction, without the tension that almost inevitably accompanies a number of people having to agree. It is not a rule over free and equal persons. A slave is a part, subordinate, without reason. A child is much the same but is capable of growing into a responsible adult and is thus educated with this end in mind.[23] (The wife is also a subordinate, but not to the degree of the slave or child. See, for instance, *NE* 1134b8-18, 1160b32-1161a2.) Aristotle believes that these parts are incapable of leading separate, independent lives.

Turning to the second question—What holds the household together?—we find that the answer is not justice, but friendship or affection (*philia*).[24] All family relationships of affection contribute to the unity of the household. They are natural and closer than most other types of friendship.

The closeness of family friendships make for a tight unity, and the authority of one gives this unity a single direction—the aim of which is the fulfillment of daily needs: food, shelter, procreation, etc. Slaves, children, and even most women, in Aristotle's view, could not achieve these without the head of the household. But this sort of unity is not appropriate to a city. The unity of the city must be less than the unity of the household (*Pol.* 1261a16-22).

Aristotle must (at least in part) mean that the rule of the household is not appropriate to the city (as we see at *Pol.* 1252a7-16), and related to this, that the parts of the city must be more independent than the parts of the household. This is supported by a passage from *NE* V 6: "There is no injustice unconditionally (*haplôs*) in relation to what is one's own; one's possession, and one's child until he is old enough and separated, is as it were a part of oneself (*meros hautou*)" (1134b9-11). A child is not separate (or independent); he is ruled by his father completely and is thus in a sense a part of another human.[25] This rule is appropriate to the household and contributes to its unity. It is not, however, the model of rule for the city—political rule.[26]

Aristotle's most important discussion of political rule is found in *Pol.* VII 14, where he says:

> if some people were as different from others as we believe gods and heroes differ from human beings (having a great advantage in the first place in body, and second in soul, so that the superiority of the rulers is indisputable and evident to the ruled), it is clear that it would always be better for the same people to rule, and the others to be ruled, once and for all. But since this is not easy to achieve . . . , it is evident that for many reasons it is necessary for all in like manner to share in ruling and being ruled in turn. For equality is [or consists in] the same thing for similar persons, and it is difficult to maintain the constitution established contrary to justice. . . . Nevertheless, that the rulers should differ from the ruled is indisputable. . . . Nature has provided the distinction [between rulers and ruled where all are equal] by making that which is the same in kind have a younger and an

older part, of which it is proper for the former to be ruled and the latter to
rule (*Pol.* 1332b16-38; see 1325b7-10).

Aristotle says that rulers can differ from the ruled among equals if the
older rule the younger. This is his recommendation for the best city. But even
where this is not practiced, there would be some differences between the rulers
and the ruled among equals, for the rulers "seek differences in outward appear-
ance, in forms of address, and in honors received" (*Pol.* 1259b7-8). But the
important point is that (slaves, children, and women aside) the differences between human beings are usually not that great; at least they are nothing like the
differences between the philosopher-kings and the other citizens in the *Republic.*[27] Thus justice (and reciprocal equality) demands that political rule—rule
among equals—not be a rule of subordination, like mastery or paternal rule,
and that unlike mastery or paternal rule, all citizens have some say in how the
city is run.

Before discussing the importance of this independence in Aristotle's citizens, let us remind ourselves of what the *Republic* said about the rulers and the
ruled. Plato created a sharp distinction between the rulers and the ruled. The
rulers are philosophers, the ruled are not. The rulers possess philosophical
knowledge—real knowledge, the ruled have opinions only. These differences
are natural, and because of them, the ruled are not capable of ruling themselves: they are "the ruled" by nature. This is made clear in *Rep.* IX:

> Why do you think vulgar and manual labor bring reproach? Or shall we say
> it is for any other reason than that when the best part is by nature so weak in
> someone, it cannot rule the beasts in him, but can only serve them, and can
> learn only the things that flatter them? . . . Therefore, in order that such a
> person be ruled by something similar to what rules the best person, we say
> that he ought to be the slave of that best person who has the divine rule
> within himself. It is not to harm the slave that we think he ought to be ruled
> . . . , but because it is better for all to be ruled by what is divine and prudent
> (*phronimou*), especially when one has it as one's own within oneself, but if
> not, then imposed from outside, so that as far as possible all will be alike
> and friends, governed by the same thing (590c-d).

Aristotle rejects all of this. It is proper for slaves, but not for normal, adult
human beings, who in the best circumstances should retain a great deal of independence. But why is independence desirable? There are, basically, two answers. First, independence is needed for human beings to live the fullest life
possible; and second, independence is necessary if the city is to function at its
best.

Let us look at the first of these. Nussbaum (1980, 418) writes that:

By nature we, or most of us, are endowed with the ability to use reason to organize our lives and plan for our futures. Aristotle argues that the active exercise of practical reason in planning a life is a deep need of each being endowed with reason and that to subdue him to the wishes of another is to deny him the conditions of a good and self-respecting life.

Men have reason, and they must use it to its fullest if they are to live truly human lives. An independent man uses his reason and acts accordingly; the reasoning and planning of others are not forced upon him.[28] (More will be said about human rational capacities shortly.)

Nussbaum (1980, 423) mentions another (though related) reason connected to the life of the individual.

[A]lthough the good may be objective . . . , the *choice* of the good must come from within and not by dictation from without. All reflective men might choose the same good life; but what makes each of them a *good man* is that he is the one who chooses it. And what is more, it will not count as a *good life* for him unless it is a life chosen by his own practical reason: prohairesis enters centrally into the specification of the good life itself.

Moral virtues do not come to us naturally; and although they involve habit (*NE* 1103a14-19), they are essentially a matter of choice (*NE* 1105a31-33). Eliminate the independence that enables humans to make choices, and virtue will be eliminated.

Jonathan Barnes (1990, 251-52) rejects this argument:

There is a familiar theme from the *Ethica*. Roughly: we achieve *eudaimonia* only if we act virtuously; we act virtuously only if we act *kata proairesin*; we act *kata proairesin* only if we act *hekontes*; we act *hekontes* only if we act freely. Hence *eudaimonia*—which is the end of the State no less than of the individual—has freedom as a precondition; and Aristotle must therefore have inclined toward a libertarian, or at least a liberal, position. This argument depends on a childish confusion. For the freedom which *eudaimonia* requires is not political liberty.

True, the claim that a man must act *kata proairesin* and thus *hekontes* if he is to act virtuously and possess *eudaimonia* does not force Aristotle to accept a libertarian or liberal position. It does, however, require at the very least that the city not act for a person, plan his life, force him to do some things and not others, etc., in every sphere of his life. Thus, although the above claim does not compel Aristotle to accept liberalism, it does force him (if he is consistent) to reject totalitarianism (which Barnes sees him tending toward). (See Miller [1983, 29-30].)

Let us now look at how independence contributes to the best rule of a city. According to Aristotle, wisdom (*sophia*, and thus surely *philosophia*) is not the essential ingredient of political science, that rational capacity most fitted for decisions concerning the city. Thus the rule of the city is not the domain of a small group of philosophers. In all normal humans there is a functioning rational part of the soul; and the appetitive part of the soul, though nonrational and often in conflict with the rational part, can obey reason. The intellectual virtue most important in this regard is *phronêsis*. *Phronêsis* "is a true state with (or involving) reason (*hexin alêthê meta logou*) [or perhaps as Irwin translates it, 'a state of grasping the truth, involving reason'], concerned with action regarding what is good or bad for human beings" (*NE* 1140b4-6). Aristotle offers politicians (especially leaders like Pericles) and household managers as examples of those who use *phronêsis*.

At the beginning of *NE* VI 8, Aristotle discusses the relationship between *phronêsis* and political science (*politikê*).

> Political science and *phronêsis* are the same state, but their being is not the same. Of *phronêsis* concerning the city, the ruling part is legislative science (*nomothetikê*), while the part concerned with particulars has the name common to both, i.e., political science. This part deals with action and deliberation, for the decree is to be acted on as the last thing [reached in deliberation]. This is why these people alone are *said* to take part in politics, for they alone act in the way that manual laborers act (1141b23-29).

We can set out the parts of political science in the following way:

Political science (= *phronêsis* concerning the city)

Legislative science: "Political science":
the ruling part   concerned with particulars
                              (involves action and deliberation)[29]

Continuing the above quote from *NE* VI 8:

> *Phronêsis* seems most of all to be that type which is concerned with the individual himself, and this part has the name common to both, i.e., *phronêsis*. Of the other parts, one is household management, another legislation, another political science, and of this last, one part is deliberative and another judicial" (1141b29-33).

The parts of *phronêsis* can be set out in the following way:

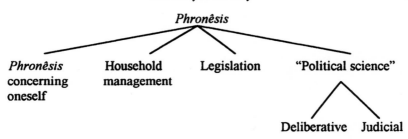

The right half of this diagram (legislation and "political science") corresponds to the diagram of political science above. Later Aristotle seems to suggest that everyone should have at least some concern for oneself, household management, and the city (*NE* 1142a7-10). This last would require at least some degree of *phronêsis* concerning legislation and/or "political science."

In *Pol.* III 4, Aristotle says that

> since the city is made up of unlike [parts or persons] . . . , the virtue of all the citizens is necessarily not one, just as in a chorus [the "virtue" or excellence] of the leader and of the followers is not [one]. . . . But will there be a case in which the virtue of the excellent citizen and the excellent man is the same? We claim that the excellent ruler is good and *phronimon*, while the [excellent] citizen is not *necessarily phronimon* (1277a5-16).

The major difference between the ruler and the ruled in this context is that the ruler will possess *phronêsis*. But I think what Aristotle has in mind is this: The virtue of the ruler is *phronêsis* in the full sense, including political science (in the broad sense of the term). Only Pericles and the like will have the knowledge necessary to make laws and propose decrees, and the ability to act on that knowledge in all the particular situations in which a city finds itself. They will know best which laws should be passed and when they should be applied. But the nonruler will (in most cases) still have a form of *phronêsis*. He will have it concerning himself and his household, and he might also have some form of it concerning the city. Such a citizen should not be left out of politics, for he will have something to say that may be of value.

This suggests that the type of *phronêsis* concerning the city that the non-ruler will possess does not include legislation, but does include some degree or form of "political science" (narrowly understood). This is confirmed by a very interesting chapter—*Pol.* III 11—where Aristotle examines the ways in which it is best for the multitude to have a say in the running of the city. Aristotle says that it is not safe for the multitude to share in the greatest offices (one reason being that their imprudence [*aphrosunê*] may lead them to err).

> But to give them no part and for them to have no share is a cause for alarm, for when there are many who are without honor [or prerogatives, *atimoi*] and poor, that city is necessarily filled with enemies. Thus, it remains for them to share in deliberating and judging (*bouleuesthai kai krinein*). This is why Solon and some other legislators arrange to have them choose and audit officials, but do not allow them to rule alone. For all of them when brought together have an adequate [or sufficient or competent] perception (*hikanên aisthêsin*) and when mixed with those who are better, they benefit cities . . . (1281b25-36).

This fits in nicely with the two parts of "political science" (narrowly understood): the deliberative and the judicial. And it suggests that the multitude tends to possess at least a narrow form of *phronêsis* concerning the city.[30]

There are two advantages to giving the multitude a part in ruling: (1) It avoids a situation that could give rise to factional conflict, namely, leaving many citizens entirely out of politics.[31] (2) The "adequate perception" of the multitude contributes something to the running of the city.

We now have a good idea of how household rule differs from political rule, i.e., how the latter requires independent citizens, whereas the former is rule over unequal, dependent people. But what about familial friendship—the "glue" that holds the household together? How does it differ from what we find in the city? First, justice and reciprocal equality have a role to play in keeping the city together, but play little or no role in a household (which depends on familial affection). Second, the kinds of friendship found in households are very close, and are mostly between unequals (which cannot be the case among equal citizens in a city). But is there a special kind of friendship among citizens—civic friendship—and is it as close as the friendships found in households? This question can be answered sufficiently only later, in chapter 4.

The Unity of an Alliance

It remains to investigate the kind of multitude that has less unity than the city: the alliance.

Most of the features of the alliance were covered earlier: The parts of an alliance are the same in kind—it is an aggregate of homogeneous members (e.g., cities). These parts are separate or separable and basically, to some degree, independent communities. An alliance becomes greater with an increase in the number of its parts, not in the number of different kinds of parts.[32] The aim of an alliance—military usefulness—is rather limited.

Pol. III 9 provides some information on the nature of alliances. If cities A and B are both members of the same alliance, this does not imply that the citizens of A care about the moral character of the citizens of B; their only concern is that the citizens of B not act unjustly toward them, i.e., that they do not violate the treaty or compact that has brought them both together and made them "allies." This is all the compact is concerned with: guarding against the committing of injustices. (E.g., if according to the treaty, A will come to the aid of B in the event that B is attacked, as a citizen of B, I am concerned with the character of the citizens of A only to the extent that they are just in carrying out their side of the bargain if my city should be attacked.) In addition, a city functions the same *qua* city whether it is part of an alliance or not. Being part of an alliance does not change what they are or how they function, it only makes their living and functioning safer (*Pol.* 1280b1-33).

In *Pol.* III 9, shortly after the section mentioned above, Aristotle suggests that what makes a city a city (and thus different from an alliance) is (at least in part) friendship (1280b38-39). This does not mean that an alliance is not characterized by *any* type of friendship. In *NE* VIII 4, Aristotle says: "people also call friends those who are friends due to utility, just as cities are, for alliances between cities seem to be for the sake of advantage . . ." (1157a25-28). The two features of the friendship of utility that should be kept in mind are: (1) one feels affection for a friend of this kind not because of the character of the person, but because there is some gain or benefit involved; (2) the friendship comes to an end when the parties are no longer useful to each other (*NE* 1156a10-21).

In conclusion, what is the one thing the parts of an alliance are related to? There is nothing even analogous to a form holding them together (like a constitution, for instance), for there are no common offices with powers over the whole alliance (*Pol.* 1280a40-b1). An alliance is one—a unity—because every member of an alliance is "related to" one treaty or compact. And what holds an alliance together? The answer is twofold: justice and friendship. The justice that in part holds alliances together is a strict justice (embodied in the treaty), according to which city A will stand by the treaty if city B does so as well. The friendship that helps hold an alliance together is a very weak form of the friendship of utility. The citizens of cities A and B feel mutual goodwill toward each other in this limited respect: citizens A wish citizens B well in whatever endeavors may ultimately strengthen them and help them aid city A, and vice versa. This friendship comes to an end (or begins to) when the alliance comes to an end, i.e., when there is nothing else to gain from the other member. It is clear in Aristotle's mind that if there were a greater concern among the parts of an alliance for the character of the individuals involved, the unity would be a tighter one. Without such a concern, one part of an alliance is bound to view the other parts as "other" and foreign.

There is nothing wrong with calling an alliance a unity, in Aristotle's view, but it is a loose unity indeed. In attempting to discover the unity of the city, it represents the lower limit: the city must have more unity than an alliance. But there is not much to add at this point. We shall come to find out that the major differences between the unity of the city and that of an alliance are that the city has an internal structure (analogous to the form of a natural substance), which the alliance lacks, and that the city has a fuller conception of justice and friendship than an alliance. (But more on this later in this chapter and in chapter 4.)

The Unity of a City

Let us, at last, ask of the city the two questions we asked of the other communities: (1) What is the one thing that each part of a city is related to? (2) What is it that holds a city together? Answering these questions will provide us with a clearer picture of the unity of the city.

First, the one thing the parts of the city—the citizens—are related to (or possess) that makes the city one is its constitution. This is the arrangement (*taxin*) or form (*eidos*) that orders the citizens through a certain conception of justice, laws, education, etc.[33] (See *Pol.* 1276b1-8, 1274b38-39; *NE* 1195a40-b1.) This is analogous to the way a form orders matter. It is much more extensive—and creates a much tighter unity—than the compact or treaty that creates an alliance. (See *Pol.* 1276b1-13.) On the other hand, the unity it produces is not as great as that found in a household or substance. The ordering of the citizens of a city by its constitution is not the ordering found in a household—it is not based on a monarchy. (Kingship is of course an exception.) Nor is it the ordering found in natural substances—it is not based on a substantial form. For as we have seen, unlike a substance and its form, the parts of a city can rid themselves of one constitution and create another. And the cause of the city's remaining one city is not the constitution as such (or completely), but (at least in part) the choice of each of the citizens. In the case of a natural substance, of course, the source of the substance's unity (and continuity) is internal, i.e., it is the form of the thing itself.

Second, what is it that holds a city together? The answer is friendship and justice. The city requires some form of friendship to hold it together, a form of friendship we might expect to find somewhere between the very close familial friendships of the household and the rather weak friendship of utility found among members of an alliance. But I shall postpone my discussion of Aristotle's views on civic friendship until chapter 4, where I discuss the criticisms of the communism of women and children (which leads naturally into a discussion of civic friendship). Instead I turn to justice (and reciprocal equality), which Aristotle stresses in *Pol.* II 2.

Aristotle claims (at *Pol.* II 2, 1261a29-31) that "reciprocal equality preserves cities," and he sends us to "the *Ethics*" for more on reciprocal equality. Aristotle's major discussion of reciprocity (and political justice) is found in *NE*

V 5-6 (=*EE* IV 5-6). The first point to make is that proportional reciprocity, not strictly equal reciprocity, is what holds cities together (*NE* 1132b31-34; see 1131a29). There are two kinds of "exchanges" that require reciprocal equality and preserve cities.

The first is the exchange of goods (e.g., builders, shoemakers, and doctors exchanging their goods and services). Though they are different, reciprocal equality makes justice in exchange possible. This, Aristotle says, holds people together (*sunechei*), and by it the city stays together (*summenei*). "Let A be a builder, B a shoemaker, C a house, D a shoe. The builder, then, must get from the shoemaker the shoemaker's product, and must give him his own product in return" (*NE* 1133a7-10). A strictly equal reciprocity would demand, say, the exchange of a house for a pair of shoes, but a city (or any other community or business) could not survive on such a principle. A proportion must be found by which a house can be said to equal so many shoes. Only then is an exchange possible. And here, money is the equalizer. It makes possible the exchange of all kinds of different goods between all kinds of different people. The only way a strictly equal reciprocity would be possible is if people produced the same things. "For no community comes to be from two doctors, but from a doctor and a farmer, and in general from people who are different and unequal, but who must be equalized" (*NE* 1133a16-18).

But the exchange between carpenters, doctors, etc., is not the only, or even the primary, exchange Aristotle has in mind. As much of the remainder of *Pol.* II 2 will bear out, the relationship and "exchange" between the rulers and the ruled is most important. This brings us to *NE* V 6, where Aristotle discusses political justice, which is "found among companions in a life that aims at self-sufficiency, who are free and either proportionately or numerically equal" (1134a26-28).

But how does reciprocal equality preserve cities? In the books on friendship, Aristotle suggests that preservation through proportional reciprocity occurs when all the parties involved are satisfied with the exchanges. (See especially *EE* 1243b15-37 and *NE* 1163b32-1164a2.) And we get a similar picture in the *Politics*. In *Pol.* II 9, he writes that "if a constitution is going to be preserved, all the parts of the city have to want it to exist and remain the same" (1270b21-22). In *Pol.* III 12, he says that people agree that equals should be treated equally, and unequals unequally, but they disagree about the standard by which equality is judged. Some think citizenship and freedom are all that matters (the democratic attitude); others think wealth alone matters (the oligarchic attitude); and still others think virtue alone is important (the aristocratic attitude) (*Pol.* 1282b17-23). When people disagree about the type of justice that exists in a particular city, then they engage in factional conflict, or at least the potential for it is there (*Pol.* 1301a37-39).[34]

In *Pol.* II 2, having stated that reciprocal equality preserves cities, Aristotle goes on to say that "even among the free and equal this is necessary, for all cannot rule at the same time, but either for a year, or according to some other order or term. And it follows in this way that all rule, just as if the shoemakers and carpenters changed places and the same people were not always shoemakers and carpenters" (1261a32-37). The first "this" in this passage refers both to the fact that the unity of the city must come to be out of human beings differing in kind, and to reciprocal equality. One follows from the other. So even in a city where the people are free and equal, differences are necessary, and reciprocal equality preserves the city.

This rather odd notion of carpenters and shoemakers changing places implies that Aristotle held that the rotation of rule was perhaps a dubious idea, or at least not the best method possible. "Since this way [i.e., not rotating] is also better with regard to the political community, it is clear that the same people always ruling is better, if possible" (*Pol.* 1261a37-39). Just as it is better for shoemakers and carpenters not to change places, so is it the case with rulers and ruled. But how could this ever be just when people are free and equal? As we have seen, Aristotle says that even among equal people there are the older and the younger, and it is proper for the older to rule because age brings with it wisdom, experience, emotional control, etc. (*Pol.* 1332b35-38).

Although the text of the next part (from *Pol.* II 2) is unclear, its meaning is not.[35] "But in those cases where it is not possible because all are equal according to nature, and at the same time it is just, whether the ruling is good or poor, for all to share in [ruling], [rotation] at least imitates [the same always ruling]. . . . For some rule, while others are ruled in turn, as if becoming other persons" (1261a39-b5). Aristotle is not suggesting that in all cases where people are equal according to nature, the same people always ruling is not possible. We saw above how this is possible. What he is saying is that under some circumstances, when all people are equal, it is just for them to adopt some kind of system of rotation. (And whether the ruling is good or poor is not an issue here.)

Even where people are free and equal it will be necessary for there to be different kinds of people. In some situations, the same people will always rule, and thus it is quite clear that there will be differences: the difference between the rulers and the ruled. In other situations, rulers and ruled rotate positions. But even here there are always differences, for this system imitates the same people always ruling, for at any given time there must be rulers and ruled. And if this were not enough, Aristotle adds that "different persons rule in different offices" (*Pol.* 1261b5-6).[36]

Because there are different kinds of people, something is needed to make the differences between them commensurable, thus making interactions between them possible. The answer is reciprocal equality. (This is true both in the economic and, more importantly, in the political realm.) When reciprocal equality is employed (along with the proper standard), then citizens can deal with each other in such a way that all parties come out satisfied. In this way, the city is preserved.

The Destruction of a City

To return to where we began (in *Pol.* II 2), Aristotle concludes his main argument there as follows: "It is therefore clear from this that the city is not naturally one in this way,[37] as some say, and that that which was said to be the greatest good to the city destroys cities. And yet the good of each thing preserves it" (1261b6-9). If a city has the same unity as the best city of the *Republic*, then the differences between human beings are eliminated in a very important respect. Yes, there will be carpenters, farmers, judges, shepherds, etc., in Kallipolis, but this is not the kind of difference Aristotle has in mind.[38] In the *Republic*, one group does all the thinking about the important things concerning the city. But this would at best lead to a large household. What is needed— and what is eliminated in the city of the *Republic*—are different people, all with their own experiences, their own opinions, their own *phronêsis*, their own contribution to the running of the city. This is a necessity. Without it, the city cannot function and is thus, for all practical purposes, destroyed. Or, like the hand that cannot function, it will be a city in name only. In this way, reciprocal equality preserves cities, as was said (*Pol.* 1261a30-31). Reciprocal equality demands that the rulers—those with the most or the highest level of *phronêsis*—have the most power and the greatest offices. But it also demands that the other citizens have some role in the running of the city as well (not to mention a full role in the running of their own lives). This, according to Aristotle, is just one of the things Plato fails to see.

Notes

1. At *Rep.* 462a-e and *Laws* 739c-d Plato aims at the unity of an individual. Most of the time, however, his communism seems to aim at making the city one large family or household. Of course, these two kinds of unity are not necessarily incompatible. For instance, Plato may have thought that the unity of an individual is what the city should strive for (without hoping to reach), and that this unity is best achieved or approached by organizing the city in such a way that it is as much as possible like a household.

2. After claiming the city differs from an alliance, Aristotle writes: "A city will also differ in such a way from a nation (*ethnous*) whenever the multitude is not separated into villages (*kata kômas kechôrismenoi*) but is like the Arkadians" (*Pol.* 1261a27-29).

This is an extremely difficult passage to interpret. The major questions are: What is meant by "in such a way"? What is meant by "separated into villages"? and Who are meant by "the Arkadians"? I can only touch on these issues and offer a tentative interpretation. For some fuller discussions of the different issues involved as well as the different scholarly points of view, see Newman (1887, 2:231-33), Susemihl and Hicks (1894, 217, 322-25), and Schütrumpf (1991, 2:163-66).

The "in such a way" indicates that the alliance is like the Arkadian type of nation, at least in a sense relevant to this discussion. But what sense is that? There are two possibilities: (1) a city will differ from a nation in that the city comes to be out of elements differing in kind; (2) they will differ in that the nation will be stronger by being larger. Newman (1887, 2:231) is right in thinking the second is correct, but I see no reason why the city and the nation cannot differ in both ways.

The word *ethnos* is hard to translate accurately, and this can lead to confusion. It can mean "a number of people living together," "tribe," "race," "people," or "a nation" (Liddell, Scott & Jones, s.v.). I think that given the context, it is best to translate it "nation," but it is precisely the wide range of meanings that necessitates Aristotle specifying just what kind of *ethnos* he has in mind. He is distinguishing an Arkadian type of nation (more on that shortly) from a nation in which the multitude is separated or scattered into villages. And it is the former type of nation that Aristotle claims is like an alliance. He most likely makes this distinction because no one would confuse a city with the latter type of nation, but one might with the former, as we shall see. (In addition, the former is powerful militarily [see Xenophon, *Hell.* VII 4.12-5.27], whereas the latter type is not [see Thucydides I 5].)

Who does Aristotle mean by the Arkadians? "The interpretation of the passage turns upon this" (Susemihl and Hicks [1894, 217]). By looking briefly at the history of Arkadia, I think we can better understand why Aristotle chose to mention it. Early Arkadia was "a far-flung group of communities whom geography and history alike had sundered" (Cary [1964, 88]). It was an *ethnos* made up of villages, with some degree of unity, namely tribal kinship, common religion, even common currency, etc. From time to time, leagues were formed and disbanded. "Attempts were made from the fifth century onwards to set up an Arcadian federation, but such attempts were impeded by rivalry between the two chief towns [i.e., Mantinea and Tegea]" (Sealey [1976, 16]). Around 370 B.C., several Arkadian villages were put together to form a new league (*to koinon*). (The term "alliance" [*summachia*] is, as far as I know, used only once in describing the putting together of Arkadian villages for military purposes: Xenophon *Hell.* VI 5.5. It is not an inaccurate term for the Arcadian league or federation. This indicates just how close an alliance and an Arkadian type of nation are.) This league was put together as a counterweight to Sparta, and its chief strength was manpower. (See Pausanius VIII 27.1; Xenophon *Hell.* VI 5.5.) It had some common offices (which met in a central city, e.g., Megalopolis), common funds, and of course, a common foreign policy (Susemihl and Hicks [1894, 324]). However, there was nothing like unanimity among its members. They were independent or at least desired independence. (See Pausanius VIII 27.2-5; Xenophon *Hell.* VI 5.6-7.) This league, "weakened by particularism," broke up within eight years, around 362 B.C. (Hammond and Scullard [1970, 94]; see also Susemihl and Hicks [1894, 324] and Sealey [1976, 434]), though Arcadian leagues continued to appear for some time.

So what did Aristotle mean by "Arkadia"? At best an educated guess is possible. Although he may have had in mind some particular period, for instance the events of 370-360 B.C. (which occurred not so long before the writing of the *Politics*), I believe he most likely had the whole history of Arkadia in mind. Arkadia was a loosely held together "nation" that from time to time had a bit more organization than usual, even some common offices (which is not a normal feature of alliances), perhaps located in a central city. In *Pol.* II 2, Aristotle probably mentions Arkadia after alliances to stave off a possible objection. What he wanted to say was something like this: "In case any of you think that a nation like Arkadia (as opposed to just a race of people occupying roughly the same territory) has more unity than an alliance, and thus that the Arkadian type of nation has a unity approaching that of a city, think again. Despite its traditional ties and some common offices, in the end it still possesses the same kind of unity as an alliance, for its aim is military strength alone. And if you want additional evidence, just see how quickly these alliances tend to break up."

3. For more on the connection between unities and wholes, see *Met.* 1016b11-17, 1052a22-31.

4. On physical (natural) continuity, see *Met.* 1015b36-1016a17, 1052a19-20, 1069a5-8; *Phys.* 227a13-16.

5. Points (2) and (3) are related, and although they are not controversial, I should say something in support of them.

According to Aristotle, the parts of an animal exist for the sake of the whole animal and are, in the deepest sense, ontologically *of* their particular organism. In *PA* I 1, Aristotle says that one should not, when discussing animals, begin with material explanations. Rather, "we should say that since this is what it is to be a man, therefore he has these [parts]; for he cannot be [a man] without these parts" (640a34-36; see 639b12-15). And there are many examples of parts being the way they are for the sake of the *bios* of some particular animal. Gotthelf (1987) gives two such examples:

> Bone and certain other hard materials are for the sake of supporting flesh or its analogue, itself necessary to all animals as the organ of the defining sense of touch. . . . [And] Why must all animals have a place [stomach(s)] for unconcoted food ready for concoction and a place for the residue of concoction prior to its expulsion? The answer clearly must be first that: "It is not possible to be (*einai*) or to grow (*auxanesthai*) without food" (655b30-2) (177, 177n31, 182).

See also *PA* II 13 for eyes and eyelids; 658b34-659a36 for the elephant's trunk; and 662a34-b17 for bird beaks. This is not to say that matter and necessity have no role to play in explanation. See *PA* 639b20-31, 640b35ff., 642a9ff., III 2.

Another way of saying that the parts of an animal are ontologically *of* the whole animal is to describe them as *dunameis*. (See the *Met.* V 26 and VII 16 passages discussed above.)

6. Of course, if I leave a city (i.e., break my civic ties with it) I am no longer a citizen of that city, but I do not thereby lose my capacity for citizenship. I can become a citizen of another city (it is at least possible) and function in the appropriate manner. I am not in any way a citizen in name only.

7. What is involved here is the fact that a group of people can be organized in different ways according to different constitutions. How this contributes to the unity of the city will be discussed later.

8. As will become clear, this is not to suggest that one could become a philosopher living a life totally outside of the city. One must be nurtured within a city and utilize the leisure that only a city can provide.

9. *Allou* here and throughout, and *hautou* (which we will come across shortly), are genitives of possession, i.e., "of another" = "belongs to another," "of oneself" = "belongs to oneself."

At 1254a10, one can read either *holôs* or *haplôs*, though there is more support in the manuscripts for the former. See the apparatus in Dreizehnter (1970, 7).

10. Cf. *Pol.* 1255b11: "The slave is in some sense a part of the master."

11. To say that a freeman belongs to no one else and exists for himself, whereas the opposite is the case for the slave, most emphatically does not imply (for Aristotle) that the freeman is one who does whatever he wants, whereas the slave does not. On the contrary, the freeman—unlike the slave—lives a well-ordered (i.e., moral and law-abiding) life, whereas a slave does not. (See *Met.* 1075a19-22.)

12. For an excellent discussion of the different senses of priority in Aristotle, and which types might plausibly be used in explaining the *Pol.* I 2 passage, see Miller (1995, 45-56). In the end, however, I disagree with Miller's interpretation in that I accept the priority-by-nature (what he calls priority by separability) interpretation, but claim that it does *not* lead to the view that the city is, or is significantly like, an organism.

13. It is worth noting that at *Pol.* 1253a7, Aristotle compares a man separated from his city to an isolated piece in "checkers." We cannot infer anything about the ontological status of the city from *this* analogy either.

14. Keyt (1987, 77-78) and Miller (1995, 49-53) also use this example.

15. Keyt (1987, 77-78) makes this same distinction.

16. Let me stress that this is not an issue of genetics or "cyclopology" and anthropology. In using the cyclops as an example, I am assuming that there is nothing inherent in Polyphemos, say, that makes him less than human; his only problem (as far as we are concerned) is that he has lived his life entirely outside of any city and thus lacks the capacity to live a full human life.

17. I say "the opportunity to live such a life" because not every person in the city, and not even every citizen, will in the end live full human lives. Most will not, or will at best approach such a life. Some will fall short of a good life through a moral failure of some kind. For others, such a life is ruled out because they have to live in such a way

that they do not have the leisure that the good life requires (e.g., farmers). Some attempts to live a full life will be impaired due to a poorly established constitution. Etc.

18. Aristotle claims that there are, however, some aspects of one's life that are so important to the life of the city that the city must have the final word and the individual must regard himself, in a sense, as belonging to the city and not to himself. I have in mind Aristotle's argument for public (as against private) education at *Pol.* 1337a21-30. (This passage is discussed in chapter 5.)

19. See *Pol.* 1261a18. Here, Aristotle calls only the city a multitude by nature, but it is clear that what he says applies to other communities as well.

20. From now on I shall write "related to," but this should be taken as shorthand for the "doing, possessing, being affected by, or being related to" mentioned in *Met.* V 6.

21. As we shall see, these two questions are intimately connected.

22. See especially *NE* VIII 11-12, 1167b33-1168a5, 1180b3-7; *Pol.* 1252a7-9, 1255b19-20, 1259b10-17.

23. These claims about the slave and the child will be supported shortly. But see *Pol.* I 4, 12-13.

24. See *NE* 1134b8-18, 1138b5-13, 1159b35-1160a7; *MM* 1194b5-13. The "justice" among family members is not justice in the sense of political justice, which exists only among equals. It is homonymous with political justice (*MM* 1194b5-13). Thus the household does not really rely on justice to hold it together. The relationships among family members are closer than those among fellow citizens or strangers. (This is not to say that we can never use "justice" when discussing family relationships. On the contrary, because they are so close, it is true, for instance, that striking one's father is more unjust than striking anyone else [*NE* 1159b35-1160a7]).

25. It should be stressed that a child is very much like a part of his parent(s), until he grows older and is capable of living a separate (i.e., independent) life. In this sense, a household is analogous to a natural substance in a strong way, given that an arm, for instance, is by its very nature a part of the animal of which it is a part and cannot exist independently.

26. There is an exception to Aristotle's claim that political rule should not be modeled on household rule, namely kingship. For a king rules his subjects in the way a father rules his children. (See, for example, *Pol.* 1252b19-22, 1285b29-32.)

27. Annas (1981, 178) and Nichols (1987, 159) have pointed out the interesting and seemingly paradoxical fact that the best city of the *Republic* involves both too great a unity and too much disparity among the citizens.

28. For textual support, see Nussbaum (1980, 417-19).

29. Cooper (1986, 35-36) remarks that political science

has two branches, corresponding to the distinction between universal and particular . . . : legislative [science] concerns universals (i.e., it speaks in very general terms about broad matters of principle, settling by law the constitutional forms and other basic arrangements of the state), while political [science], taken now in the narrow sense, deals with particulars . . . : it concerns itself with day-to-day management of political affairs—for example, getting the people to outfit a fleet, or build a temple, or vote a distribution of food, and so on.

30. Aristotle writes that "the diner is the better judge of a meal, not the cook" (*Pol.* 1282a20-23; see *Pol.* III 4).

31. Toward the end of *Pol.* II 5, Aristotle writes:

> It is dangerous how Socrates appoints the rulers. For he makes it so the same people are always ruling. But this becomes a cause of factional conflict even among those possessing no worth, and more so with high-spirited and warlike men. That it was necessary for him to make the same people rulers is clear. For the gold from the gods is not mixed in the souls of some at some times while in others at other times, but always in the same. He says that, directly when born, to some gold is mixed, and to others silver, and bronze and iron to those who are going to be craftsmen and farmers (1264b6-15).

32. Alliances are made up of homogeneous parts in the sense that each part of an alliance is the same kind of thing, for instance, a city. This is not meant to suggest that all the parts of an alliance contribute the same amount or provide the same benefit. (NATO, to give a contemporary example, is made up of homogeneous parts—nations—yet Belgium, for instance, cannot contribute as much as the United States, though it does contribute something.) Nor is it meant to suggest that no one part has more power or authority, nor that no other parts are subordinate to a more powerful one. (See, for example, the old Warsaw Pact.)

33. Aristotle rarely uses *eidos* to describe a constitution (*Pol.* 1276b7 being the only place, or one of the few, where he does so), preferring instead *taxin* (e.g., *Pol.* 1274b38).

34. Aristotle devotes *Pol.* V 8-9 to the discussion of the preservation of constitutions. What preserves a constitution is the opposite of what destroys it (and factional conflict is most of all what destroys it). He gives a lot of advice on how to preserve constitutions, which depends very much on the type of constitution in question. In general, though, he says that preservation requires the right kind of justice in the right situation (e.g., sometimes equality based on citizenship should be used, and sometimes equality based on merit), which in turn requires *phronêsis* and moderation, and therefore education.

35. I follow Dreizehnter's text, and omit the worst line (which he brackets).

36. Newman (1887, 2:235) writes: "So inseparable is differentiation from the State, that when its members are alike and equal, differences are conjured up not only between rulers and ruled, but even among rulers."

37. "In this way" means "entirely one" (1261a15), "unified too much" (1261b10), "one to the highest degree" (1261b16), "completely one" (1261b20), "one in every sense" (1263b31).

38. This is in answer to the objection of Mulgan (1977, 29), who writes that Aristotle's criticism that Plato makes the city too much of a unity "hardly counts against the *Republic*, the whole structure of which depends on a rigid division of labour." (See also Saunders [1992, 103] and [1995, 109].)

Chapter Three

Unity and Self-Sufficiency

> Aristotle seems to separate unity and self-sufficiency from one another.
> Proclus, *Commentary on Plato's Republic* (2: 363.18)

Aristotle believes that too much unity is not desirable in a city because it makes the city what it is not, thereby destroying the city. At the end of *Pol.* II 2, Aristotle describes another way in which "seeking to unify (*henoun*) the city too much is not better" (1261b10-11). He claims that too much unity reduces a city's self-sufficiency since a multitude of different people with different functions is required for self-sufficiency. Unfortunately, neither Aristotle in this passage (nor scholars of Aristotle commenting on it[1]) say much that reveals what he means. Most tend to think his point is obvious—and, some would add, obviously wrongheaded as an objection to Plato. Saunders (1992, 103) writes: "Diversity of function (as between different occupations, and between ruler and ruled) was recognized and provided for as much by Plato as by Aristotle. Much of the criticism in this chapter therefore pushes at an open door." Saunders does add, however, that "Aristotle's relationship to Plato is a rich and complex topic, and it should be stressed that on the justice of his criticisms of Plato's philosophy, and of the political theory in particular, more than one opinion is possible." In this chapter I shall present another possible opinion on Aristotle's criticism of Plato at *Pol.* 1261b10-15.

The Self-Sufficiency Argument in *Politics* II 2

Aristotle makes two points that are supposed to support his claim that too much unity is not desirable: (1) A city is more self-sufficient (*autarkesteron*) than a household, and a household is more self-sufficient than an individual

37

(*Pol.* 1261b11-12). (2) "A city tends to be [a city] when the community that comes to be from the multitude is self-sufficient" (*Pol.* 1261b12-13). Point 1 describes a comparative relationship, and Aristotle no doubt had another such relationship in mind, namely, the one mentioned at *Pol.* 1261a16-22, where he claims that an individual has more unity than a household, and a household more unity than a city. Apparently, Aristotle believes that taken together these relationships imply an inverse relationship between self-sufficiency and unity. The more there is of the one, the less there is of the other. Point 2 also suggests a connection between a high degree of self-sufficiency in the city (it is *the* self-sufficient community) and the fact that the city does not possess a high degree of unity (it comes to be from a multitude). Aristotle concludes from 1 and 2 that "If what is more self-sufficient is more choiceworthy, then what has less unity is more choiceworthy than what has more unity" (*Pol.* 1261b14-15). What is more self-sufficient is obviously more choiceworthy (see *Rhet.* 1364a5-8; *NE* 1097b7-15; *Pol.* 1253a1), thus we can conclude (by modus ponens) that what has less unity is more choiceworthy than what has more unity. This was Aristotle's aim at *Pol.* II 2, 1261b10-15.

As it stands, however, Aristotle has not leveled a successful criticism against Plato, for he has not successfully defended the idea that what has more unity is necessarily less self-sufficient, and that what is more self-sufficient necessarily has less unity. For instance, one could claim that a city occupies more space than a household, and a household more space than an individual; and that a city has less unity than a household, which has less unity than an individual. But this does not prove that there is a necessary inverse relationship between spatial extension and unity. (One could imagine a small clan occupying less space than a large household and yet possessing less unity than the household.) Moreover, even if such an inverse relationship were proved in this way, the proof would tell us nothing about *why* an increase in one leads to a decrease in the other. But surely this is crucial.

If it cannot be shown how the self-sufficiency of a city will be too little if its unity is too great, then Bornemann (1923, 130) was correct in claiming that Aristotle's argument at *Pol.* 1261b10-15 is simply an eristic frivolity. The remainder of this chapter attempts to answer the following question: How (if at all), given Aristotle's political philosophy, might one defend his claim that the high degree of unity of Kallipolis makes impossible a proper level of self-sufficiency?

Autarkeia

It will be helpful to set the historical context by discovering what, in general, is meant by *autarkeia* (self-sufficiency).[2] Unfortunately, it is used in many ways to refer to many different things, and we need to narrow this down a bit.[3] In *Pol.* II 2, Aristotle is interested most of all in the self-sufficiency of the city, and this will be our main concern. By first looking at how some others have applied *autarkeia* to the city, we shall get a better idea of the kinds of issues Aristotle is dealing with.[4]

Herodotus and Thucydides provide us with good examples of the application of self-sufficiency to cities. In Herodotus I 32, during a conversation about the most blessed men, Solon tells Croesus:

> Now it is impossible for one who is human to lay hold of [or gather together, *sullabein*] all these things [i.e., goods], just as no land (*chôrê*) is fully sufficient (*katarkeei*), providing everything by itself, but it has one thing, while it needs another. But the [land] that has the most things, this is best. And so too, no one human is self-sufficient (*autarkes*), for he has one thing, but is in need of another.

There are two points of interest: First, self-sufficiency in this view is the ability to acquire everything, or being in need of nothing. Second, self-sufficiency is impossible for both a city and an individual, for both must rely on other cities or other individuals for the things that are needed. Neither an individual nor a city can provide everything he or it needs himself or itself.

Turning to a somewhat different view of self-sufficiency, Pericles says (in the funeral oration of Thucydides, book II) that the Athenians have organized their city in such a way that "it is completely self-sufficient (*autarkestaten*) both in peace and in war" (II 36). Gomme (1956, 105-6) remarks that

> this does not imply any degree of 'self-sufficiency', in the sense of Athens, or even the empire, supplying all its own needs. On the contrary, Athens imported freely from abroad, and was proud of the fact . . . , and was particularly dependent on wheat and timber from outside the empire. . . . But it was in a position to get all that it needed, both by its industry and commerce and its military power. . . .

The Athenian pride Gomme refers to is expressed by Pericles as follows: "Because of the greatness of our city, all goods from all over the world come to us, and as a result we do not enjoy our own, familiar products more than the products of other men" (II 38). A bit later in the funeral oration Pericles boasts that individual Athenian citizens are themselves self-sufficient (II 41), and again, Gomme (1956, 127) is correct in commenting that "*autarkes* is used of the individual in the same sense in which it was used of the state in 36.3—it does not of course mean that the individual does not give anything to, nor receive anything from, another, but that he is in a position to do both."

This view of self-sufficiency is similar to Solon's in that self-sufficiency refers to the ability to acquire all the goods, or being in need of nothing. But it differs in that it includes in its conception of self-sufficiency the ability to acquire goods from the outside. For example, if a city produces no barley of its own, yet is able to acquire it through trade, then it is not in need of barley, at least not in a sense that diminishes its self-sufficiency.

Looking ahead, we can say that Aristotle agrees with Solon and Pericles when he writes, in *Pol.* VII 5, that "self-sufficiency is having all things and needing nothing" (1326b29-30).[5] We shall come to see, however, that his conception of self-sufficiency is closer to Pericles' than it is to Solon's, in that it includes the ability to acquire goods from the outside.

Self-Sufficiency in the City

Aristotle distinguishes two kinds of self-sufficiency in the city. The first is self-sufficiency with regard to life or living (*pros zôên autarkes, Pol.* 1328b17). This type of self-sufficiency is also described as self-sufficiency with regard to necessary things (*en tois anagkaiois autarkês, Pol.* 1326b4; cf. 1254b4, 1321b17) and simple self-sufficiency (*haplôs autarkê, Pol.* 1328b18; cf. 1275b21). Generally, if a city is self-sufficient with regard to living, it will lack none of the necessary things (e.g., food, shelter). The second kind of self-sufficiency in cities is self-sufficiency with regard to the good life or living well (*autarkes pros to eu zên, Pol.* 1326b8-9; cf. 1256b32, 1280b31-34). Generally, if a city is self-sufficient with regard to living well, it will lack nothing required for the good life of the city as a whole. The details of these two kinds of self-sufficiency will become clearer as we proceed.

It is important to keep in mind that these two conceptions of self-sufficiency are not mutually exclusive, describing two different kinds of city. They are meshed together rather thoroughly. True, a "city" that is self-sufficient solely with regard to living will not be self-sufficient with regard to living well (and we should perhaps not even call it a city; see *Pol.* 1280a32-33); but a city that is self-sufficient with regard to living well must also be self-sufficient with regard to living, i.e., it cannot lack the necessities of life. (See *Pol.* 1253b24-25.)

In this section I want to discover what it takes for a city to be self-sufficient. I hope to discover the nature of the self-sufficient city through an examination of what exactly such a city needs. I shall begin with a more general account, and then fill in the details.

In *Pol.* VII 1, Aristotle divides the goods into three kinds (1323a24-27): (1) external goods (e.g., wealth); (2) goods of the body (e.g., health); (3) goods of the soul (e.g., moral virtue). All of these should be available to the best city, he says, and, as we shall find out, all cities must have some of each. (See also *NE* I 8 and *Rhet.* I 5.)

Still speaking in very general terms, there are two sorts of equipment necessary for the existence of a city: territory and a population. In the best city that one could pray for, the territory yields every sort of thing that is needed—in this manner the city would not have to depend on others in any way. But since this may not be possible, the city should lie in relation both to land and sea in such a way that it can import whatever it needs and export its surplus (*Pol.* 1326b27-39, 1327a7-10, 1327a18-20, 1327a25-28).[6] But although the city's territory should be able to produce what is needed, it should not be such that (1) it requires most of its citizens most of their time to get from the land what the city needs (for this would make the proper amount of leisure impossible); or (2) it is so overflowing in external goods that citizens would tend to be (or would be tempted to be) immoderate. (In general, see *Pol.* VII 11.) Clearly, Aristotle is looking toward both living and living well.

As for population, Aristotle says a city cannot be too small in population or it will lack self-sufficiency (i.e., it will not have enough people to produce all of the goods it needs). Nor can it be too large, or it will be capable of self-sufficiency with regard to living only, but will not properly be a city. Such a "city" will not be well managed (*Pol.* 1326a25-b7).

> With a view to judging [or making decisions, *krinein*] about matters of justice and with a view to distributing offices according to worth, it is necessary for the citizens to know each other with respect to what kind of people they are. Where this does not happen to be the case, the matters concerning offices and judging must necessarily be handled poorly. . . . Thus, it is clear that the best limit [or definition, *horos*] of a city is this: the greatest number of people with a view to self-sufficiency of life that is readily surveyable (*eusunoptos*) (*Pol.* 1326b14-24).[7]

Continuing to discuss the population (in a sense), let us look at the necessary conditions or parts of the city that are functions or activities (*erga*), and the people who perform them.[8] Aristotle lists these in *Pol.* VII 8: (1) sustenance, and thus a multitude of farmers, etc.;[9] (2) arts/crafts (*technas*), and thus artisans or craftsmen; (3) arms, and thus a fighting element; (4) a ready supply of funds, and thus a well-off element; (5) superintendence connected with the divine, and thus priests; (6) judgment (and thus judges) of advantageous things and just things—those things affecting how citizens relate to each other (1328b2-23). These are the functions that every city needs. "For the city is not a chance multitude, but one self-sufficient with a view to life, as we assert. But if the city happens to be lacking in any of these, it is impossible for this community to be simply self-sufficient" (1328b15-19).

In order to show the complexity of the needs of the city, I should like to look more closely at what Aristotle considers the most important of these activities or functions: the political ones. At the beginning of *Pol.* IV 14, Aristotle says that there are three parts that all cities must possess (and concerning which the lawgiver must be knowledgeable): the deliberative part, the executive part (i.e., the part connected with offices), and the judicial or adjudicative part (1297b37-1298a3). They are discussed in *Pol.* IV 14-16.

The deliberative element has authority over laws; war and peace (including treaties and alliances); judicial cases with severe penalties (i.e., death, exile, or confiscation of property); and the auditing of officials (*Pol.* 1298a3-7).

In *Pol.* IV 15, discussing the executive element, Aristotle says that of the types of superintendence, "those are to be called offices most of all to which are assigned deliberation and judgment concerning certain matters (*peri tinôn*),[10] and command, but most of all this last, for to command is more characteristic of ruling" (1299a25-27). Aristotle discusses the various executive institutions in much greater detail in *Pol.* VI 8. He mentions three types of offices: necessary offices, the highest necessary offices, and offices peculiar to the best and most prosperous cities. There are six necessary offices:[11] (1) superintendence of the market;[12] (2) superintendence of public and private property in town;[13] (3) field management;[14] (4) office of receivers;[15] (5) office of recorders;[16] (6) the office connected with prisoners[17] (1321b12-1322a29). Next come the five higher necessary offices: (1) superintendence of military matters;[18] (2) office of accountants; (3) council;[19] (4) superintendence of things connected with the gods;[20] (5) the office concerned with sacrifices not assigned by law to the priests (*Pol.* 1322a29-b29). Finally, Aristotle mentions (without much detail) the offices found among cities that have the most leisure, prosperity, and orderliness: (1) manager of women; (2) law guardian: the aristocratic version of the third of the higher necessary offices (see *Pol.* 1322b12-17, 1323a8); (3) manager of children; (4) exercise official; (5) superintendent connected with gymnastic and Dionysiac contests, and any other spectacles of this sort[21] (1322b37-1323a6).

Aristotle discusses the judicial element in *Pol.* IV 16. There are eight kinds of court, concerned with: (1) audits; (2) anyone acting unjustly with respect to what is common; (3) what bears on the constitution; (4) disputes over fines (affecting both private persons and officials); (5) private transactions of a certain magnitude (cf. [8] below); (6) homicide, for which there are four courts;[22] (7) aliens, for which there are two courts;[23] (8) small transactions (1300b19-33).

All of these political functions will be performed by citizens and only by citizens.[24] Not all citizens will be able (or eligible) to hold every kind of office, but all or most will be able to hold political office of some kind at some time in their adult life. In fact, they will probably have to. These offices require different degrees of *phronêsis* or experience.

But citizens have another function besides the political ones. They are all (for the most part) property owners and household managers. (In the best city, every citizen will own land. See *Pol.* 1330a9-23.) The activities this involves are also a requirement of the self-sufficient city. One important function of a household manager (and, in fact, of some political rulers) is the acquisition of the goods that the household (and city) needs. Both the possession of goods, and the buying and selling of goods, are required for self-sufficiency (*Pol.* 1321b14-18, 1329a17-19; *NE* 1133b6-10). To examine these activities in more detail, we need to look at Aristotle's views on expertise in business (*chrêmatistikê*), discussed most fully in *Pol.* I 8-11.[25]

There are three kinds or parts of expertise in business. The first—expertise in business in its most proper sense (*Pol.* 1258b20)—is acquisitive expertise (*ktêtikê*). There are natural and unnatural versions of this. Natural acquisitive expertise is concerned with acquiring sustenance through natural means. It is limited in that it aims at self-sufficiency, not limitless profit. (See *Pol.* 1256a19-b32, 1257b30-31, 1258a16-18, 1258a34-38; *Oec.* 1343a25-b6.) Unnatural acquisitive expertise is concerned with gaining limitless profit through any means. (See *Pol.* 1256b40-1257a7, 1258a15.) Experience in the following three parts of natural acquisitive expertise is useful for household managers and political rulers: (1) the raising of livestock;[26] (2) farming; (3) the raising of animals besides livestock (e.g., beekeeping). These are the major ways in which sustenance is acquired. (See *Pol.* 1258b12-20; *Oec.* 1343a25-b6.)

The second part or kind of expertise in business is expertise in exchange (*metablêtikê*). The unnatural (and unjustified) version of this is expertise in commerce (*kapêlikê*),[27] the aim of which is limitless profit. Barter, import and export between cities, and exchange within cities based on money, are all justified versions of exchange (*allagê*) when they are performed for the sake of acquiring necessities, use what is in surplus, and aim at self-sufficiency. Although they are not contrary to nature, they cannot be considered natural, Aristotle believes, since they are a form of exchange and (in the case of the last two) based on money. (See *Pol.* 1257a14-b14, 1321b14-18, 1327a19-20, 1327a25-31; *NE* 1133a19-b16.)

There are three parts of expertise in exchange useful for household managers and political rulers (*Pol.* 1258b21-27): (1) trade (*emporia*), which is the greatest part of exchange and which is further divided into three parts: (a) provisioning ships, (b) transport, (c) marketing (2) money lending (*tokismos*);[28] (3) wage labor (*mistharnia*) of two kinds: skilled and unskilled (*Pol.* 1337b4-15).

Aristotle mentions a third kind of expertise in business, which is a mix between the first and the second. It concerns things from the earth that are unfruitful but useful, e.g., mining and lumbering. (See *Pol.* 1258b27-33; cf. *Oec.* 1343a25-b6.) We can infer from what we have seen so far that although this type is not fully natural, it is a justified form of acquiring goods when it is limited and aims at self-sufficiency. In addition, we can infer that it would be useful for some household managers and political rulers to know something about it.

I should like to look more closely at the idea (so far undefended) that household managers and political rulers should show an interest in, and know something about, expertise in business. Clearly it is useful, Aristotle says, for both household managers and (some) political rulers[29] to know something about expertise in business, since both the household and the city need revenues. Of course, the kind of expertise in business that should interest them is the natural sort, which is limited, aiming at useful and necessary goods—those required for self-sufficiency. They are not concerned with acquisition in the sense of making or producing goods, but with properly using what is provided by others. (See *Pol.* 1256a10-12, 1256b26-39, 1258a21-35, 1259a33-36; *MM* 1192a15-20; but cf. *Oec.* 1343a5-9.)

It is still not clear what household managers and political rulers need to know, but Aristotle's discussion of the raising of animals gives us a clue (*Pol.* 1258b12-16). There he tells us that the household manager and political ruler do not need to know the entire science of animal husbandry, beekeeping, etc. But, with a view to acquiring what the household or city needs, they should know which animals are most profitable at which places under which conditions, etc. In general, each has "to see that the art of acquiring wealth is practiced, without exercising it himself" (Susemihl and Hicks [1894, 187]).[30] Subordinates, or those totally outside their sphere of influence, would make the various products and see that they were available, but the household managers and (appropriate) rulers would have to know whether the products were good, were getting to the household or public storerooms efficiently, etc. And this requires knowledge or skill of some kind.[31]

This completes the presentation of the conditions and "parts" required for self-sufficiency. I should next like to investigate what types of people Aristotle thinks should perform the various functions that have been described.

In summary, let us enumerate the types of people needed for a city to be self-sufficient: (1) officials, deliberators, judges, etc.; (2) military men; (3) priests; (4) well-off people; (5) artisans; (6) merchants, moneylenders, etc.; (7) farmers, fisherman, lumberjacks, etc. Those in categories 1-3 must of course be citizens (see *Pol.* 1329a2-5, 1329a27-34). Category 4 is no doubt made up primarily of citizens, but there would certainly be resident aliens who would properly fit into this category. In any case, it is not so important. As for 5, most likely some will be citizens (the most artful), and some certainly cannot be (the most vulgar, who, at least in the best city, should not be citizens). (See *Pol.*

1258b25-27, 1258b35-39, 1277b36, 1278a8-13, 1278a20-25, 1328b39-41, 1329a19-21.) Finally, neither 6 nor 7 should consist of citizens.[32]

We have a good idea who are and who are not the citizens. What I want to stress, however, is that the division between the two does not represent a mutually exclusive division in the affairs with which people concern themselves. True, farmers and moneylenders should not, according to Aristotle, have a say in the governing of the city (at least not in the best city), nor should they take part in religious rites, etc. But the reverse is not the case. As I hope has been made clear, citizens—both in their role as heads of households, and as rulers of the city—will have to have some knowledge of, and take an interest in, merchants, farmers, beekeepers, blacksmiths, etc. This is the key to understanding *Pol.* 1261b10-15. As we shall come to see, the problem with the best city of the *Republic* is (briefly) an improper connection between the ruling class and the affairs of the lower class (caused by an improper conception of the unity of the city).

The city, in order to be self-sufficient, must have a diverse population—made up of citizens and noncitizens—consisting in farmers, auditors, shepherds, judges, accountants, fishermen, craftsmen, soldiers, merchants, sailors, beekeepers, superintendents, etc. (This diverse group of people is able to interact because of reciprocal equality, a system of laws, and exchange in the marketplace based on money.) But to be truly self-sufficient, a city must also possess leisure (*scholê*). But leisure by itself is not enough. Nomads have leisure, but they do not live full human lives (*Pol.* 1256a32); and the Spartans ruined themselves because they did not know what to do with their leisure (*Pol.* 1271b5; cf. 1334a4-10). So it is what a city *does* with its leisure that is crucial. But "while we agree that a city that is to be finely governed ought to have leisure from necessary things, in what way it ought to have this is not easy to grasp" (*Pol.* 1269a34-36). Let us attempt to grasp this.

There are, basically, three "political" advantages to having (a great deal of) leisure: (1) It allows more time to be spent on political activity—both going to the Assembly, and more serious political activity, like deliberation (*Pol.* 1300a3, 1329a1). (2) It leads to trust and the knowledge of one another that is necessary for good government (*Pol.* 1313b2-6; cf. *EE* 1244b19-21). (3) As we saw above, it allows for special offices (*Pol.* 1322b37-1323a9). But leisure is not only or even primarily beneficial because it is conducive to good government. It has other advantages as well. History has shown, Aristotle says, that leisure leads to science (*Met.* 981b13-29) and every sort of learning (*Pol.* 1341a28). And as we shall see shortly, leisure promotes virtue and makes the highest activities possible (e.g., philosophy).

In *Pol.* VII 14, Aristotle says:

> All of life can be divided into lack of leisure [or occupation, *ascholia*] and leisure, and war and peace, and of actions some aim at what is necessary and useful, while others aim at what is noble. . . . War must be for the sake of peace, occupation for the sake of leisure, what is necessary and useful for the sake of what is noble. . . . One should be able to work [i.e., be occupied] and go to war, but should rather remain at peace and be at leisure, and one should act with a view to what is necessary and useful, but with a view to what is noble more so (1333a30-b3; cf. 1334a4-10).

In the following chapter he tells us that because many necessary things must be present if a city is to have leisure, the city must possess both those virtues that aim at the necessary things and those that aim at leisure. We need courage, endurance, moderation, and justice with a view to occupation, i.e., with a view to acquiring and using necessary things, and protecting them in times of war; and we need moderation, justice, and philosophy with a view to leisure so that we use our leisure and good fortune properly, without becoming arrogant and immoderate—slaves to the abundance of goods we possess (*Pol.* 1334a11-15).

In *Pol.* VIII 3, Aristotle introduces the notion of "noble leisure." He says that education aims at being occupied in the correct manner and at being at leisure in a noble fashion (*scholazein kalôs*) (1337b29-35). Now we must be clear about what counts as an occupation and what counts as an activity proper to noble leisure. Aristotle says that leisure—unlike mere play—involves pleasure, happiness, and living blessedly. And this is not possible for those who are occupied (insofar as they are occupied) since occupations aim at some necessary end. So there should be education with a view to leisure—with a view to things done for their own sake (e.g., music). But household management and political activities are occupations.

> The activity of the practical virtues is exhibited in politics and in affairs of war, and actions concerning these seem to be unleisurely. Actions in war are completely so, for no one chooses to fight a war for the sake of fighting a war. . . . But political action is also unleisurely, and beyond taking part in political activity itself, this type of action seeks to gain power and honors, or at least happiness for the politician himself and for his fellow citizens, which is different from political science, and is clearly sought as being different. So among virtuous actions, political actions and actions in war are superior in nobility and greatness, but they are unleisurely, aim at some end, and are not choiceworthy for their own sake (*NE* 1177b6-18).

The same can be said for the activities involved in household management, which also aim at some higher end.

In summary, farmers, shepherds, craftsmen, etc., will not possess any real leisure. Their whole lives will be spent on their occupations, and on play and relaxation. Leisure, we saw, was conducive to political activity and household management, but this is not the noblest end of leisure. Noble leisure should aim at such pursuits as music, poetry, and philosophy. Thus leisure makes possible a further nurturing of virtue. Now the division between occupation and leisure is not a strict one. Someone could be occupied part of the time, and devote the rest to activities at which noble leisure properly aims. (See *Oec.* 1345a16-17.) But it is also possible to be fully free of all occupation. As Susemihl and Hicks (1894, 542) state, Aristotle has in mind the "leisure worthy of a really free man, such as he attains when his political duties have been performed, or such as he always possesses, provided he is pecuniarily independent, and leads a life of true study or contemplation." Education must therefore aim at occupation and leisure, and the virtue proper to both.

We now have a good idea of the importance and role of leisure in the city. But where does this fit into our discussion of self-sufficiency? A city and its citizens will not have leisure: (1) if they have little property (*Pol.* 1291b26; cf. 1326b31); and/or (2) if everyone has to work to live (*Pol.* 1292b28, 1329b31). (On both points, see *Pol.* 1293a5, 1300a3.) What is needed are time and wealth: time to perform the activities proper to noble leisure, and wealth to finance these activities and (in some cases) maintain those performing them. But this requires a high degree of self-sufficiency. If a city can acquire all the goods it needs so efficiently that it produces a great deal of wealth and leaves time for the noblest activities, improving political activity, better household management, all kinds of arts, etc., it will be self-sufficient. And not only will it be self-sufficient with a view to living, with leisure for the highest human activities—assuming it uses its leisure properly (which requires certain conditions, e.g., a system of education, familial ties, friendships and associations of all kinds)—it will also be self-sufficient with a view to living well. (See *Pol.* 1253b24-25.) In fact, I submit that this is what self-sufficiency with a view to living well is. One can imagine a city efficient enough to feed, cloth, shelter, defend, etc., all its inhabitants, but with no time or wealth left over for noble activities, or with no view of the proper end at which to aim if they did have the means, time, and wealth. (See *Pol.* 1331b26-34.) Such a city would be self-sufficient only with a view to living.

We are now in a position to understand what Aristotle means when he says a self-sufficient city has everything and is in need of nothing. Obviously, he does not mean such a city has every single thing, not even every sort of thing (e.g., a city does not have to have wheat to be self-sufficient, so long as it has or can acquire something—barley for instance—with which to make bread). What it must have are all the necessities of life—food, clothing, etc.—in some form, and all the activities that correspond to these things and make them possible;[33] and this includes political functions or activities, and certain virtuous activities (justice, moderation, *phronêsis*). (A city characterized by these things alone would be self-sufficient only with a view to living.) In addition, the city must have enough of these things, and these activities must be performed efficiently enough, such that the most people possible have leisure and the means to use it properly. And if they do use their leisure properly, then the city will also "possess" excellent citizens (*Pol.* 1332a32-34) and noble activities. This is self-sufficiency with a view to living well.[34]

Self-sufficiency with a view to living well requires certain external conditions (e.g., territory), but also a number of different types of people. In the case of noncitizens, they must know their trade or business and perform their work adequately. But more is required of citizens. In the last chapter, I demonstrated that most citizens must have some degree of *phronêsis* for playing some part in the running of the city and for running their households. In addition, we saw earlier in this chapter that they will have to possess some knowledge of the acquisition and use of possessions. Now, of course, the most important citizens are those with the most *phronêsis*—those who hold the highest offices. But these are not the only men who are (nor is this the only type of intellectual virtue that is) crucial. The fate of the city does not depend entirely on the knowledge of those in the highest offices. A city functioning properly also depends on its citizens being individuals with a high degree of autonomy: men with full capabilities, tangible goods, and the ability, as heads of household, to run their own lives and the lives of their families.

Now in what sense is a city more self-sufficient than a household or an individual? Neither an individual separated from a city (by nature) nor a pre-city household will be able to come up with the leisure required for the best sort of life. Individuals can be self-sufficient, but only in the context of a life lived in a city.[35] And this is why self-sufficiency is the goal of the city. It makes the city complete. Nothing else is needed for the happiness and good life of the human beings within it. The greatest number of people possible (but most likely not all) will be able to live the noblest life possible. (See *Pol.* 1325a5-10, 1325a31-34, 1325b14-16.)

Self-Sufficiency in the *Republic*

Plato in the *Republic* (like Aristotle after him) holds that "a city comes into being because each of us is not self-sufficient, but is in need of much" (369b). And he is aware of the need for many parts. There will be rulers, auxiliaries, and the iron and bronze men; and within the lower class there will be much diversity, for the city requires farmers, weavers, cobblers, housebuilders, craftsmen and smiths of all kinds, all sorts of herdsmen, merchants, "men who know the business of the sea," tradesmen, wage earners, cooks, barbers, artists, musicians, doctors, etc. (*Rep.* 369e-373d).

Given that Plato recognizes that a diversity of men is needed in order for the city to be self-sufficient, what could be the nature of Aristotle's criticism? As I hope will become clear, we cannot answer this question until we have examined in greater detail the *Republic*'s position on the relationship between the gold and silver classes on the one hand, and the bronze and iron class on the other, beginning with their respective educations.

Much is uncertain concerning the early education of the lower class—i.e., the iron and bronze class (see *Pol.* 1264a36-40). Nevertheless, it is clear that starting very early, the members of the lower class receive an education different from that of the guardians. (See the appendix, n. 4.) And obviously, the lower class does not receive the intense philosophical education of *Rep.* VII. Those who make up the lower class will be educated in their crafts, besides receiving a moral training of sorts. (See Reeve [1988, 189-91].) It seems that if they know their respective jobs, each performs only his own job, and they are relatively moderate, then as far as Plato is concerned the lower classes will be able to produce what the city needs (i.e., the necessities, such as food and shelter) for themselves and the guardians (*Rep.* 369c-370a). The guardians, however, receive an elaborate education aimed at the characteristics that will enable them to guard well.[36] And (with some minor exceptions that will be discussed later) this education does not attach any importance to the practical affairs of the city. This is confirmed by the education of the philosopher-kings-to-be. For example, Socrates tells Glaucon that the future rulers should not study arithmetic (*logistikē*) the way private citizens do, but instead they should aim at "seeing the nature of number with thought itself, not attending to it for the sake of buying and selling like merchants or tradesmen, but for the sake of war and for the sake of turning the soul itself with ease from becoming to truth and being" (*Rep.* 525b-c).

Basically, we know that the rulers (the philosophers) and the auxiliaries (the warriors) rule, and the iron and bronze men are ruled. But what do the rulers know about the affairs of the ruled? Their education does not seem to have given them much information of this sort. The auxiliaries will have no acquaintance with households, property, markets, farming, etc. (*Rep.* 415d-417a; cf. 423a). And the same must go for the philosophers as well, for many of the same reasons, but especially because one cannot become a real philosopher *and* run a household and make money (*Rep.* 497e-498a). But without "knowledge" of the workings of the lower class, what is the ruler's claim to rule? What sort of knowledge does he have? Our first hint at an answer is found in an important passage in *Rep.* IV, at the point where the interlocutors are searching for wisdom in the city. There, Socrates says, and Glaucon agrees, that the city is truly wise, not due to the knowledge possessed by carpenters, smiths, farmers, etc., but because of the guardians' special knowledge and good counsel (*Rep.* 428b-e).

The rulers will not have "knowledge" of the particular skills of the lower class, but an entirely different type of knowledge. This knowledge is explained more fully in books V-VII of the *Republic*. The philosopher has a desire for the whole of wisdom, but this does not include a desire to learn sensible things—those things seen and heard. The philosopher has real knowledge—not opinions—and that means knowledge of the Forms, and particularly of the Form of the Good. This, more than anything else, distinguishes philosophers from nonphilosophers (*Rep.* 475b-480a, 484b-c, 504d-505b). Plato also writes that the rulers will possess experience (*Rep.* 484d). But experience in or of what? (This is the point at which their education might seem to be of great help in enabling them to rule the affairs of the city.) At a young age they will be taken on horseback to be spectators of war (*Rep.* 537a). But more importantly, the philosopher-kings-to-be, for fifteen years (until they are fifty) will

> be compelled to rule in matters of warfare and in whatever other offices are proper for young men, so that they will not be behind the others in experience. And in these things as well they must be put to the test to see if they will stand firm when pulled in every which way or move aside (*Rep.* 539e-540a).

In general, how will the philosophers rule with their special type of knowledge? Presenting the Allegory of the Cave, Plato says that once a person has grasped the Forms, when he goes back down the cave, he can (given time to adjust) see ten thousand times better than the others there (*Rep.* 519c-521b). Earlier Plato said the city would be perfectly ordered if a guardian who knows the Forms oversees it (*Rep.* 506a-b). Why? We know the Forms will somehow provide the rulers with a pattern (*paradeigma*) for making and preserving fine, just, and good laws (*Rep.* 484c-d), and ordering the city:

> Once [the philosophers] have seen the Good itself, using this as a pattern, each in his turn must order (*kosmein*) city, private men, and themselves for the rest of their lives. Now for the most part they spend their time in philosophy, but when a person's turn comes, he labors in politics and rules for the sake of the city, not as though he were doing what is fine, but that which is necessary (*Rep.* 540a-b).

But how can the philosophers use the Forms as patterns for ordering the city? Here the *Republic* does not give us much help. We were told that after wiping the slate clean, the rulers must come up with an outline shape of the constitution, and then look back and forth between the Forms and actual human beings to fill in the details (*Rep.* 501a-c). Adam (1902, 2:79) quite rightly remarks that the result "is not a compromise between for example Athens and the World of Ideas, but something as near the latter as the limitations of earthly existence will allow—in other words such a polity as is described in the *Republic*." But this could only serve as a pattern for the original ordering of the city. But what about the day-to-day administration of the city? All we know is that according to Plato rulers will be quite capable of such rule as long as they know the connection between the Form of the Good and the particular instances of justice, prudence, etc. (*Rep.* 504e-506b).

What does the *Republic* tell us about the way (and the degree to which) the rulers will rule the affairs of the lower class? We have seen that the members of the lower class are the ruled by nature, and that with the Forms the rulers must rule themselves, the city, and private men (i.e., the ruled). Specifically, they will supervise craftsmen for the same reason they must supervise poets (*Rep.* 401b-d). They will guard against wealth and poverty (letting no one become too wealthy or too poor) since an excess of wealth and poverty leads to luxury, idleness, innovation, inefficiency, illiberality, and wrongdoing (*Rep.* 421d-422a); and, they will judge lawsuits, making sure that no one has what belongs to another (*Rep.* 433e).

What about laws concerning the marketplace—i.e., laws concerning contracts, fraud, libel, duties and taxes, harbor regulations, disputes and complaints, etc.? In an interesting passage (*Rep.* 425c-e; cf. 465b-c; see Adam [1902, 1:219]), the suggestion seems to be that Socrates and his companions in the dialogue will not bother going through the laws that must be passed to govern the activities of the marketplace. Such laws will be taken care of by the rulers in the city. But this passage claims that this should not be a difficult task if "the laws we described before" are preserved: most likely the supervision of poetry; the community of property, women, and children among guardians; laws against innovation; and limits against extreme wealth and poverty. It is easier to keep order in the market if the men in it are moderate. (See *Pol.* 1264a29-32.)

Aristotle's Criticism

Given this picture of Kallipolis, why does Aristotle think that it (with its high degree of unity) will lack or have little self-sufficiency? For a city to be self-sufficient (especially with a view to living well) it must have all the required conditions, parts, and activities, and the parts must perform the necessary activities efficiently and properly. Let us assume Kallipolis has all the required conditions and parts.[37] Why, according to Aristotle, can they not function properly?

In the last chapter, we saw that the high degree of unity in the city of the *Republic* required (according to Plato) a strict division between the rulers and the ruled, with absolute political power resting with the rulers.[38] The rulers must be total rulers, and rulers by nature, whereas the ruled were the ruled by nature. The ruled were not independent; they could neither plan their lives for themselves nor live their lives by their own judgment. They were something analogous to children or slaves. The total rule by the rulers (it was hoped) gave the city one direction and avoided the fragmentation that might result in having a city full of independent citizens each planning his own life. The essential difference between the rulers and the ruled lies in their knowledge (or lack thereof). The rulers have a knowledge of the Forms and experience of a certain kind but little or no knowledge of the affairs of the lower class. They rule without concern for the "knowledge," opinions, and experiences of the nongold citizens. The members of the lower class are in some sense heads of households, and, where applicable, they are responsible for their trades or crafts. The ruled would know their own tasks, but they would have to be directed by the rulers. (See Reeve [1988, 208].)

Why according to Aristotle would the rulers and/or the ruled not be able to function properly? Let us first look at the rulers. We saw that for Aristotle, even some of the political rulers in the higher offices needed at least some knowledge of the workings of the "economy" to rule well. (As Aristotle says at the beginning of *Pol.* I 11, experience is especially necessary in the case of business expertise and household management.) In addition, the rulers' job was made easier by the contributions of other citizens, who shared in the rule of the city (employing their own knowledge, experiences, opinions, etc.) and who, for the most part, were responsible for their own lives and the lives of their families. In the *Republic*, the rulers must rule all the affairs of the city, as well as, in a sense, the individual lives of all nongold citizens. They rely wholly on their own knowledge, which consists primarily of the knowledge of the Forms. But Aristotle maintains that even if the Forms did exist, they would be useless in practical affairs:

> Even if the good predicated in common is some one thing, or something separate, itself in itself, clearly it could not be acted upon or possessed by man, but that is the sort of thing we are seeking. . . . Difficult, too, is how a weaver or carpenter will be benefited with a view to his own craft from knowing this Good itself, or how the man who has gazed on the Form itself will be a better doctor or general (*NE* 1096b32-1097a13).

The same surely goes for rulers as well, for perhaps the most important aspect of *phronêsis* in the political realm is the ability to act in particular situations.

Aristotle's criticism in *Pol.* II 2, however, is not essentially aimed at the Forms. I believe he would argue that even with a correct epistemology, Plato's guardians would not be able to properly run the city (without the help of the knowledge, opinions, and experience of the nonrulers) as well as order the lives of all its citizens. The fact that they will rely on the Forms—which, even if they do exist, are useless in practical affairs—only exacerbates their problems.

But what about the experience the philosophers gained during their education between the ages 35 and 50? Would they not have acquired exactly that sort of practical knowledge I have claimed they lack? I do not think so. Plato probably had in mind many of the offices mentioned by Aristotle—any that would be proper for young men to hold. But which offices could these men adequately hold without previous experience in the affairs of the city and without becoming corrupted through an acquaintance with low things like markets and farms? (Cf. *Pol.* 1333a6-11.) Perhaps the offices of recorders, receivers, and auditors, and maybe some others; but this would produce nothing like the experience they would need to rule fully once they turned fifty. Nor is it enough to run the city, for who will fill the other offices? So it seems the rulers would be entirely unable to conduct the practical affairs of the city.[39] And if the ruled had to be directed by the rulers, who were unable to function properly, it might be the case that the ruled would not be able to provide sufficient "wages" for the rulers, thus precluding or severely limiting the leisure required by the philosophers and others for the noblest activities. (See Saxonhouse [1982, 213-14].)

The unity of the best city of the *Republic* depends on one "voice" (that of the rulers, armed with a knowledge of the Forms) commanding the whole of the city. Everyone else is, in an important sense, mute. The city is not a harmonious chorus of independent voices. But as Aristotle writes later in *Pol.* II, as a city becomes too much of a unity "it will cease to be [a city], but while it remains [a city] . . . , it will be a worse one, just as if someone were to make a harmony a unison or a rhythm a single beat" (1263b32-35; see Stalley [1991, 190]). According to Aristotle, what is needed for self-sufficiency with a view to living well is a *full complement* of whole, independent men with various abilities. But this is incompatible with a high degree of unity, since a highly unified city does not contain independent men leading their own lives, but rather citizens more like slaves than freemen. (In a somewhat different context, Aristotle writes that it is impossible "for a city that deserves to be so called to be slavish by nature, for the city is self-sufficient, but what is slavish is not self-sufficient" [*Pol.* 1291a8-10].)

The best city of the *Republic*, because of its extreme unity and for the reasons stated earlier, will not be able to produce all the necessities of life, will lack a sufficient amount of leisure, and will thus severely lack self-sufficiency, both with a view to living and living well.

Notes

1. This passage is generally given very limited treatment in commentaries on the *Politics* and in articles on Aristotle's criticisms of Plato's *Republic*. Newman (1887, 1: 160-61, 2:236) and Susemihl and Hicks (1894, 221) say next to nothing. Schütrumpf devotes less than half a page to the passage (1991, 2:173). See also Stalley (1991, 190), Saxonhouse (1982, 213-14), and Simpson (1991, 106).

2. Etymologically, *autarkeia* is derived from two words: *autos* and *arkeô*. Liddell, Scott, and Jones gives three kinds of definition for *arkeô*. First, it means "ward off" or "defend," and thus "assist" or "succor." This gives rise to two other sorts of definition, one being "make good" or "achieve," the other "to be strong enough," "suffice," "to be sufficient or enough," etc. Thus, on purely etymological grounds we should expect *autarkeia* to mean something like "the ability to defend oneself," "the ability to achieve or secure enough for or by oneself," "self-sufficiency." And indeed, *autarkeia* is generally translated by "self-sufficiency" or, less frequently, "independence." (I shall be translating it by "self- sufficiency.")

3. The terms *autarkeia* and *autarkês* were applied to many things, both profound and mundane. First, I shall give some of the uses found outside of Aristotle. They have been applied to: happiness (thus, for instance, if one is happy one does not need anything else; see Plato, *Philebus* 67a, and Demosthenes, *Funeral Speech* 14); god ([Plato], *Definitions* 411a); trees, barley, and wheat seeds (Theophrastus, *History of Plants* IV 13.5, VIII 6.1); a human body during the plague (Thucydides II 51.3); the young stomachs or bowels of children (Aeschylus, *Libation Bearers* 757); the cosmos (Plato, *Tim.* 33d); fire and water (Hippocrates, *Regimen* I 3, 35); ruddle (Theophrastus, *On Stones* VIII [53]); a shout (Sophocles *Oedipus at Colonus* 1057); abilities (Demosthenes, *On the Embassy* 340); a remedy (Hippocrates, *Regime in Acute Diseases* 1, 5, and *Regimen* I 2); a discovery (Hippocrates, *Regimen* I 2); and decrees (Demosthenes, *Third Olynthiac* 19). In most cases the meanings are "self-sufficient," "independent," "sufficient," or "enough." Some other meanings, which should not surprise us, are "complete" and "strong enough." The two strangest (and earliest) uses are: calling the young stomachs or bowels of children *autarkês* (which means they depend on the will of no one, neither the child nor the nurse), as well as a shout (which, since "sufficient shout" does not fit the context, probably means "vigorous shout").

In Aristotle, the range of meanings or applications is quite broad as well. He applies the terms to: arguments (*NE* 1179b4; cf. *Top.* 102a16, 150b23); god (*DC* 279a21); certain animals (*GA* 732a17, 776b8); a king (*NE* 1160b4); certain sciences (*NE* 1112b1); and happiness and the good (*NE* 1097b7-15, X 7-8, *Rhet.* 1360b15-1362a36). This last is especially important in Aristotle and is crucial for understanding his conception of the self-sufficiency of individuals. Yet however important this issue is, it shall not concern us, for we are interested in the self-sufficiency of the city.

4. There is very little on self-sufficiency in the *Republic*, but see 369b, 387d.

5. By itself this definition is inadequate and ambiguous. For instance, self-sufficiency cannot literally mean having every single thing or lacking in nothing at all. What precisely Aristotle means we shall discover later.

6. Hammond (1986, 9), describing the geography of Greece, writes:

> The characteristics of Greece . . . are common to almost all the cantons of the Greek mainland and to many of the islands. Each canton may be said to represent a cross-section of Greece, comprising highland, lowland, and coast. Laconia, Attica, and Acarnania, for example, possess arable plains and olive-growing lowlands as well as summer pastures and forest-clad highlands. The same is true of such islands, for example, as Cephallenia, Crete, and Rhodes. Within each canton and within many of the islands there are often several small plains, each surrounded with its own orbit of highland and lowland. Each canton or island, and several smaller units of territory within them, are self-sufficing in the primary products necessary for subsistence. This peculiarity favoured the growth of numerous states, which each possessed the first elements of self-sufficiency.

7. See Newman (1887, 3:346–49). He writes that "*eusunoptos* must apparently mean 'easily within the view of the magistrates and the citizens.'" On the general quality of the population required, see *Pol.* 1327b29-33 and *Rhet.* 1360b30-1361a11.

8. In an important chapter, *Pol.* VII 8, Aristotle sets out the necessary conditions and parts of the city. He begins by saying that what are (merely) necessary conditions are not to be considered parts of the city (1328a21-25). But a bit later he says that what we call the parts of the city would seem to include those things that must of necessity be present in the city (1328b3-4). Now this certainly appears inconsistent, but I think Aristotle has something like the following in mind: The city requires many necessary conditions. These are not parts of the city, but most of them do imply the existence of certain classes of people whom we do regard as parts of the city (at least in one sense of the term "part"). For instance, one necessary condition, sustenance, implies the existence of farmers, and farmers can be considered a part of the city.

Filmer (1949, 200-201) writes: "Aristotle is not resolved how many parts to make of a city, or how many combinations of those parts; and therefore in his reckoning of them, he differs from himself, sometimes makes more, sometimes fewer parts." Aristotle sometimes seems to consider everyone who has a function in the city a part of the city; at other times, only citizens seem to count (see *Pol.* 1327b9). But this need not concern us too much, for we are only interested in what the self-sufficient city requires (whether we call these requirements parts or not).

9. Newman (1887, 3:376) writes: "Aristotle forgets that herdsmen, fishermen, and hunters are also providers of food."

10. Newman (1887, 4:258) writes: "Aristotle adds *peri tinôn* because a magistry has a definite, not an indefinite sphere of competence."

11. Many of these offices are known by more than one name. Notes 12-23 simply give further descriptions of the offices, thus the reader may wish to skip them.

12. This office is concerned with agreements and orderliness.

13. This office is concerned with orderliness, prevention of boundary disputes, maintenance of public property, etc. It has many parts, sometimes relegated to other officials.

14. This office is basically the same as (2), but is concerned with the country (*chôra*) and other things outside the town.

15. That office "which receives revenues from common things, guards them, and distributes them to each administrative element" (*Pol.* 1321b30-33).

16. This office registers private agreements and judgments from the court. Indictments and initiations of suits are also registered by this office.

17. The most difficult office, but very necessary. Difficult because it is a bad job, so no one will want to do it; necessary because justice must be done. Because it is a bad job, it should be broken up and given to other officials, and the guarding should be left for the young. Newman (1887, 4:556) writes: "Aristotle does not mention the title of this magistry, as he mentions those of others—perhaps because he is in effect proposing its abolition. . . ."

18. The office concerned with the defense of the city. It is made up of many offices, e.g., generals, admirals, cavalry commanders.

19. This office is the most authoritative. It introduces measures and has authority over the final disposition.

20. This is held, for example, by priests. The duties of this office include guarding temples and maintaining sacred buildings.

21. Newman (1887, 4: 566-67) suggests, and this is quite plausible, that (1) sees to it that women observe orderliness, (2) does the same for males, and (3) for boys. He says (4) keeps order in the gymnasium and (5) might refer to the manager of such events.

22. The four types of homicide court concern: (1) premeditated murder; (2) involuntary manslaughter; (3) cases in which it is agreed that homicide was committed but there is no agreement as to what is just; (4) homicide by those who have been exiled for homicide and have returned.

23. The two courts for aliens concern cases involving aliens against aliens and aliens against citizens.

24. Hopefully, there will be one person per office and no one person will have to hold more than one office (*Pol.* 1273a8-9; cf. 1261b5-6).

25. There are several interpretive problems with *Pol.* I 8-11. There is a problem with terminology, especially with the term *chrêmatistikê*, which had many meanings in Aristotle's time. Also, it is unclear whether what follows are parts or kinds of *chrêmatistikê*. (See *Pol.* 1256a15-16, 1256b40-1257a2, 1257b33-1258a14, Newman [1887, 2:165], and Susemihl and Hicks [1894, 209-11].) Finally, there is some doubt as to whether *Pol.* I 11 is genuine and, if so, how it fits into the rest of book I. (See Newman [1887, 2:196-98] and Lord [1984, 17, 246n45].)

26. Aristotle elaborates on what one needs to know about livestock:

> What kinds are most profitable and where and how; for example, what kind of [course should be followed in the] acquisition of (*ktêsis poia tis*, see Newman [1887, 2:200]) horses or cattle or sheep, and similarly with the other animals, for one ought to be experienced about which are most profitable compared with each other, and which kinds in which places, since different kinds do better in different areas (*Pol.* 1258b12-16).

27. See *Pol.* 1257a17-19, 1257b1-5, 1257b23-30, 1258a38-b2. We should perhaps add to this usury (*obolostatikê*). (See *Pol.* 1258b2-8). Expertise in commerce can be viewed as a part of, or equal to, unnatural acquisitive expertise. (See *Pol.* 1258a38-b2.)

28. According to Liddell, Scott & Jones, *tokismos* is "the practice of usury," and *obolostatikê* is "the trade of the petty usurer, usury." Perhaps *tokismos* is the more general term, referring to both the justified type of money lending (for instance, the financial backing of a business venture) and the unjustified type, whereas *obolostatikê* is the lending of small amounts at high interest—the (or one kind of) unjustified money lending. (See *NE* 1121b34.)

29. I say "some," because of course not every single office holder will have to know these things, though many will, e.g., superintendents of the marketplace. Such knowledge would no doubt also prove useful in the Assembly or Council.

30. See *PA* 639a3-14, *NE* 1181a17-b3, *Pol.* 1341b9-14, 1342a19-21.

31. *Oeconomica* I 6 mentions with favor three methods of preserving wealth (the Persian, the Lakonian and the Athenian), but most of the chapter is devoted to the Persian method, which is clearly regarded as the most important.

> The Persian system involves everything being organized and [the head of the household] watching over everything himself . . . ; for no one attends to what belongs to others and what is his own in the same way, so that as far as possible, one ought to attend to everything oneself. . . . Some things should be inspected by [the head of the household] himself, others by his wife, since the work of household management is divided between them. These inspections ought to be made a few times only in small households, but more often in households where overseers are employed (1344b34-1345a8).

The standard view is that this work was not written by Aristotle, but (in the case of book I, which is the most Aristotelian) by an early Peripatetic, possibly Theophrastus. Whoever the author was, it was heavily influenced by Aristotle, *Pol.* I, and Xenophon, *Oeconomica*.

32. On (6), see *Pol.* 1258b35-39, 1328b39-41, 1337b8-15, *Oec.* 1343a28-b1. As for (7), farmers are not necessarily vulgar, but they lack leisure; the others lack leisure and are vulgar, slavish, and/or ignoble. See *Pol.* 1258b25-39, 1278a11-13, 1278a20-21, 1319a20-24, 1328b39-1329a2, 1329a25-26, 1330a25-30, 1332a25-30, *Oec.* 1343a25-b6.

33. Perhaps we should say all the natural goods (*ta tê phusei agatha*). See *NE* 1169b19-20.

34. Irwin (1988, 615-16n12) writes: "If the city is self-sufficient and complete, it includes within itself all the activities that constitute happiness and the necessary means for them, including the right number of people. . . . Once it has reached this stage it need not grow any further, but has reached its proper natural limit. . . ."

35. The city is more self-sufficient than the individual not simply because the city has more goods and is better equipped to get and secure them (although that is certainly part of it), but also because an individual's self-sufficiency depends on the self-sufficiency of the city.

36. See Reeve (1988, 179-80) for a list of characteristics and where they can be found in the *Republic*.

37. In *Pol.* IV 4, Aristotle criticizes the claim made by Socrates in the *Republic* (at 369d) that the city of utmost necessity would be made up of four or five men (e.g., a farmer, a weaver, a builder) (1291a10-24). Aristotle says a city of so few would not be self-sufficient, and in fact aims only at what is necessary. But this is a narrow criticism leveled solely at the protocity of *Rep.* II (the city of pigs), not at Kallipolis, which seems to have a full complement of people. (Perhaps Aristotle was prompted to make this criticism because Socrates refers to it as "the true city" [372e].)

38. In *Pol.* II 6, Aristotle (rather surprisingly?) writes that "concerning farmers and craftsmen, whether they share in rule in no way whatsoever or to some extent . . . , Socrates has not determined" (1264b34-37). Susemihl and Hicks (1894, 246) argue that the principle of the division of labor makes it quite clear that they do not share in rule at all, and I am inclined to agree (but cf. Newman [1887, 2:265]).

39. If I am right, then Aristotle's criticism of Plato at the end of *Pol.* II 2 is somewhat similar to the view, most forcefully argued by the Austrian school of economics (e.g., by Ludwig von Mises), that economic calculation is impossible under socialism. (See Waldron [1988, 6-11] and, especially, Miller [1983].) Cf. *Pol.* 1261b33-38, discussed in the following chapter.

Chapter Four

Unity and Affection

All three children were in rags; the clothes given to them by the Red Bonnet Battalion had been worn to shreds. . . . Who had been taking care of those children? No one could have said. No mother. Those savage peasant fighters, who had been dragging them from forest to forest, gave them their share of soup. That was all. The children got along as best they could. They had everyone for a master and no one for a father.

> Victor Hugo, *Ninety-Three*, part 3, book 3 (trans. Lowell Bair)

Friendships are not only compensation for the cold impersonality of public life but a vital source of personal identity. "Friends are the one thing we have which are all our own," a mathematician confided. "They are the one part of our lives where we can make our own choice completely for ourselves. We cannot do that in politics, religion, literature, work. Always, someone above influences our choice. But not with friends. We make that choice for ourselves."

> Hedrick Smith, *The Russians* (describing friendship in the former Soviet Union)

In *Pol.* II 2, Aristotle presented two arguments against the conception of the unity of the city found in the *Republic*. He next wants to show that "even if this is best—the community being to the highest degree one" (*Pol.* 1261b16-17)—it is not achieved by the means Plato proposes in the *Republic*. The correct conditions for unity (any kind of unity) are not to be found in Plato's plan for Kallipolis. The first set of criticisms of the communism of the *Republic* as a means to unity (*Pol.* II 3-4) concern friendship or affection (*philia*),[1] and are aimed particularly at the communism of women and children. A consideration of these criticisms not only provides us with some of Aristotle's reasons for

59

rejecting Platonic communism, it also sheds light on his own conception of the proper unity of the city by illuminating his theory of civic friendship.

Politics II 3 (1261b16-32): An Important Ambiguity

In the *Republic*, Plato's Socrates asks: "Is that city in which most (*pleistoi*) say 'mine' and 'not mine' about the same things in the same way the best governed city?" Glaucon responds: "By far" (*Rep.* 462c). All middle-aged adult males, for instance, will share, or say "mine" of, all young males. The latter will be "sons" to these "fathers" in common. And the affection felt will be that which is usually felt between fathers and sons. Plato believes such intense feelings in all for all will produce the most unity possible in the city, and this he says is good (*Rep.* 457c-464d).

Aristotle, with this passage in mind, says that the highest degree of unity in a city (even if that were desirable) is not proved by the argument that the most unity will come to be "if all (*pantes*) say 'mine' and 'not mine' at the same time" (*Pol.* 1261b17-19).[2] The argument is invalid, Aristotle claims, because its use of "all" is double in meaning (*ditton, Pol.* 1261b20).[3] Later in this passage he repeats his claim that "all" is double in meaning and goes on to say that it is a fallacy to use "all" in this way since it produces "contentious inferences in the arguments" (*Pol.* 1261b27-30; see *Top.* 162b3-5 and *SE* 168a25-34).

Let us look at the two meanings that, according to Aristotle, Plato fails to distinguish. The first meaning of "all" is "each taken individually," when "each individually will say the same son is his own, and the same woman, and similarly concerning property" (*Pol.* 1261b20-24). Aristotle says that this is probably how Plato wants to be understood (*Pol.* 1261b21-22), and he is right (see *Rep.* 463c-d). A person will not only call his fellow citizens "father," "brother," etc., he will also act as if they were his natural fathers, brothers, and so on.[4]

The second meaning of "all" is "all taken collectively": "But as it is, those who have women and children in common will not speak in this way [i.e., in the way Plato wants], but as all [collectively], not as each of them [individually], and similarly with property" (*Pol.* 1261b24-27). Clearly this meaning of "all" would involve, for instance, calling all males of about the same age "brother," but without the emotion and action that generally accompanies such a relationship.[5]

Let us examine how this ambiguity affects Plato's argument. Here are two versions of his argument (in abbreviated form): The argument using "all" in the first sense (A1), and the argument using "all" in the second sense (A2):

A1: If each person individually says "mine" and "not mine" at the same time about the same people, the city will have a great deal of unity—much like the unity of a family.

A2: If all collectively say "mine" and "not mine" at the same time about the same people, the city will have a great deal of unity—much like the unity of a family.

Aristotle says that A1 is fine, but impossible (*Pol.* 1261b31). That is, if each individual could *actually* treat all those older than he is as parents, and all those younger as children, etc., with all the responsibility, emotion, and activity that entails, it would be fine. It is, however, impossible. He claims that A2, on the other hand, is simply false. For "all" taken as it is in A2 is "not at all conducive to concord" (*Pol.* 1261b32). Aristotle devotes the remainder of *Pol.* II 3-4 to showing why "all" in the first sense is impossible, and in the second is not conducive to concord.

Politics II 3 (1261b32-1262a1): What Is Common Is Given the Least Care

Aristotle says that "all saying 'mine' and 'not mine' at the same time about the same things" is harmful in another way (*Pol.* 1261b32-33). That is to say, not only does it produce a fallacious argument, it has other (more tangible) problems when put into practice. Indeed, these are the major problems with the communism of women and children.

The first such problem is this: When a relatively large number of people share things in common, they tend to neglect them. "What is common to the most people gets the least care since they are concerned (*phrontizousin*) most of all with their own things, but less with the common things, or [only with] as much as falls to each [individually]" (*Pol.* 1261b33-35). Individuals sharing things in common neglect the things being shared more, "as if someone else were concerned, just as in household service many servants sometimes serve worse than fewer" (*Pol.* 1261b35-38). If I were one of many servants, I might not attend to my master (by pouring him some more wine, say): I might neglect him because I honestly believed one of the other servants must have served him already; or, I might think I can get away with not serving him (with the excuse, if caught, that I thought someone else had served him).

Aristotle infers from this that the same thing will happen among human relationships within the kind of communism of women and children advocated by Plato:

There comes to be a thousand sons to each of the citizens, and these not as [sons] of each [individually], but any chance man is equally the son of any chance man [given that they are in the relevant age groups], such that all [the "fathers"] will equally neglect them [i.e., the "sons"] (*Pol.* 1261b38-1262a1).

Aristotle is not primarily making a point about the affection felt between these "fathers" and "sons" (though he is leading up to this). Rather, he is saying here that no matter what these men might feel for their thousand "sons," they will end up neglecting them since it is quite natural (or quite tempting) to think that someone else is taking care of them.

Politics II 3 (1262a1-14):
The Fragmentation of Affection

Such neglect will, of course, affect what the "fathers" and "sons" feel for each other.

> In this sense (*houtôs*) [alone] does each say 'mine' of the citizen who is do-ing well or badly:[6] [according to] what number (*hopostos*) he [the citizen who is doing well or badly] happens to be in relation to the number [of citi-zens], i.e. [each citizen says] 'mine' or 'so-and-so's'(*tou deinos*), speaking in this manner to each of the thousand or however many the city has, and doubting this (*Pol.* 1262a1-5).[7]

Aristotle wants to say something like the following: Each citizen (of a certain age group) says of each younger male citizen (also of a certain age group): he is my son or A's son or B's son or C's son . . . or, finally, n's son (where n is the total number of "fathers").[8] Therefore he is 1/nth my son, and thus I am con-cerned with (at most) only 1/nth of his well-being (i.e., whether he is doing well or badly).[9] And the same is true of the other relations between citizens. Affection, Aristotle is saying, has not been multiplied, but divided. And from this fragmentation of affection comes a decrease in concern or care.

It is bad enough that each boy is only 1/nth of a son; what is worse, each citizen, Aristotle says, will doubt even this. Why? "For it is not clear to whom a child has been born, and having been born, whether it has survived" (*Pol.* 1262a5-6). This does not change the 1/n fraction, since each citizen must as-sume that he or A or B, etc., is the father. What it does is cast doubt by adding another factor. Each citizen will say: "this boy is 1/nth mine—assuming I fa-thered a child who survived to this age (something I can never be sure of)." (Such doubt assumes an inability to recognize one's real [i.e., biological] chil-dren. In a long digression, Aristotle discusses the consequences of both the in-ability and the ability to recognize one's real offspring under a system where women and children are common.)

Aristotle asks which is better, everyone calling a certain young man "1/nth my son" (or "1/mth my brother," etc.), or the way it is now. Nowadays, he says, the same person, depending on the relationships he has to different people, is called a son, brother, nephew, cousin, son-in-law, brother-in-law, etc.; and if not related by blood or marriage, he might still be called a clansman or tribesman; and if he is neither a relative, clansman, nor tribesman, he is still regarded as a fellow citizen. There are thus several different levels of affection or friendship. Plato wanted to get rid of this wide variety of friendships and make everyone a close relative, thus ensuring the most unity possible. (See *Rep.* 463c.) But Aristotle has replied that this does not work. A 1/nth son is for all practical purposes no son at all. Instead of close familial affection, there is no affection, for such a "son" is given no (or almost no) parental care.[10] Thus, Aristotle writes, "it is indeed better to be [someone's] own nephew than a son in this manner [i.e., everyone's son]" (*Pol.* 1262a7-14).

Politics II 3 (1262a14-24): Favoritism

The major issue in *Pol.* II 3-4 is what could be called the fragmentation of affection. But Aristotle digresses a bit to discuss the problems surrounding an issue raised earlier: the ability and inability citizens will have to recognize their own, natural offspring. Aristotle wants to show that both recognizing and failing to recognize one's own children generate problems for the communism of the *Republic*.[11]

So far we know that the average citizen (or guardian) does not know who his actual relatives are—this is why there is the doubt mentioned above. But we cannot infer from this that no one will ever recognize any of his real relatives, or at least have suspicions. Aristotle writes: "But in truth it is not possible to escape the fact that some will suspect who their own brothers, children, fathers, and mothers are. For from the resemblances, which come to the children from their parents, they necessarily find proof about each other" (*Pol.* 1262a14-18). Aristotle presents two related types of evidence in support of this claim. The first is directly related to the issue at hand (namely communism), but it is based on the second, which is a fact of nature.

The first piece of evidence is this: We know of cases where women and children are held in common, and yet resemblances are still noticed. "Some of the very ones who have written on travels about the earth[12] say this happens. For [they say] that among some [of the inhabitants] of upper Libya the women are common, yet the children born are distinguished according to resemblances" (*Pol.* 1262a18-21). Aristotle's source is probably Herodotus (IV 180), who writes that the Auseans (a Libyan tribe)

have sexual intercourse with their women in common, and they do not live
together [as couples], but have intercourse like beasts. When a woman's
child is full grown, within three months the men gather together in the same
place, and they consider the child to be of the one among the men whom the
child resembles.

The second, and in a sense more important, piece of evidence is the easily
observable fact that females (human and nonhuman alike) often produce offspring similar to one of their parents.[13] "There are also some women, [and fe-
males] of other animals, like horses and cattle, that have a natural tendency to
produce offspring similar to the parents, just like the mare in Pharsalus called
the Just" (*Pol.* 1262a21-24).[14]

But why is the possibility of the detection of family resemblances a problem? Aristotle does not say here, but he does hint at what is wrong at the end of
Pol. II 4. It seems such detection could lead to favoritism (and worst of all,
nepotism) among the guardians. Discussing some of the technical difficulties
with transferring children to different classes, Aristotle says that "those giving
and transferring [the children] necessarily know who gives [what child] to
whom" (*Pol.* 1264b28-29). This causes problems. The communism of the *Republic* requires that each citizen treat all other citizens as family members; but
if an individual citizen knows or suspects that someone is his real (i.e., natural)
parent, child, etc., this will vitiate Plato's scheme. For Aristotle believes that
humans will by nature feel greater affection for their own children, brothers,
etc., so if they know or suspect who their own relatives are, there will be an
imbalance: some citizens will feel more affection for some fellow citizens, and
less for others. This imbalance is especially problematic to Plato's communism
if, say, a gold father knowingly keeps his son—who turns out to be iron—from
being transferred to where he belongs.

Politics II 4 (1262a25-40): Impious Crimes

But however problematic the above suspicions concerning one's real relatives might be for the communism of the *Republic*, for the most part citizens
will not know who their relatives are. According to Aristotle, this ignorance
will generate two sorts of impious crimes or acts: violent ones and sexually perverse ones.

Aristotle begins *Pol.* II 4 with the following:

For those arranging this community, it is not easy to avoid such difficulties
as outrages, involuntary homicides (and voluntary[15]), fights, and verbal
abuses. None of these is holy (*hosion*) happening to fathers and mothers and
those not remote in kinship, as [distinct] from those who are remote. But

these necessarily occur more often among those who are ignorant [of whom their relatives are] than among those who are acquainted [with them]. And when they do happen, it is possible, among those who are acquainted [with them], for the lawful atonements (*tas nomizomenas . . . luseis*) to be done, but not among those who are not (1262a25-32).

Aristotle's meaning is clear enough: Because citizens will not know who their real (i.e., natural) relatives are, certain impious acts will occur more frequently—violent and abusive acts, which are unholy when committed against one's close relatives—and the city will be unable to do anything to expiate these actions. It is, however, a bit more difficult to ascertain the point of this criticism. One view, with a great deal of initial plausibility, is that Aristotle actually believes that certain actions are impious or unholy (in the religious sense), and that much ill would befall the city if the proper remedies were not initiated (or at the very least such actions are lamentable because they are impious).[16] Newman (1887, 2:241) in a note on this passage, seems to support this view. But at the end of the note, he leaves open the possibility of another kind of interpretation. "Indeed, if Bernays is right (Theophrastos über Frömmigkeit, p. 106), the Peripatetics thought little of expiatory sacrifice, so that Aristotle here may be speaking somewhat exoterically." That is, Newman admits that it is possible that Aristotle himself did not believe that certain actions were unholy in the religious sense of the term, but instead was arguing solely on the assumption that the citizenry would have such beliefs. This would not be unusual for Aristotle, who often argues dialectically, i.e., from *endoxa* ("reputable opinions").[17]

I should like to present a version of this second type of interpretation—one that takes into account Aristotle's purpose in *Pol.* II 3-4: the criticism of the communism of women and children as a means to the unity of the city. That is, I do not think Aristotle believes the holy (in the religious sense) is a legitimate moral concept. He believes, however, that most citizens do; and he believes the fact that they do, combined with the communism of women and children of the *Republic*, would diminish the unity of the city.

Aristotle rarely uses the term *hosios* (holy). We find it at *NE* 1096a16 and *Pol.* 1335b19-26, and in neither case does the term have a necessarily religious meaning.[18] Indeed, as Dover and Adkins have shown, by Aristotle's time *hosios* had many meanings, both religious and secular. For instance, it is sometimes synonymous with *dikaios*.[19] But in our passage Aristotle refers specifically to "lawful atonements," which suggests that this use of *hosios* is religious. Acts that were not *hosios* might bring pollution (*miasma*) to the city, and this pollution had to be removed through purification rites, exile, etc.[20] This must be what he means by lawful atonements. And yet this should strike us as odd, for there was, in intellectual circles, a move away from the tradi-

tional views on pollution, and Aristotle, it seems, was a part of this move-
ment.[21] For instance, according to the traditional view, a son killing his father
was an act that led to pollution (perhaps indelible pollution), no matter what
the reasons for the father's death. (See, for instance, Sophocles *Oedipus the
King* 1182-1530 passim; cf. Aeschylus *Eumenides* 652 ff., and *Seven against
Thebes* 680 ff.) Aristotle, however, when discussing the accidental killing of
one's father, calls it unfortunate (*atuches*) but makes no mention of its unholiness or the need for atonements (*MM* 1195a18-22, *NE* 1135a15-30, *EE* II 9). In
a different passage, he calls striking one's father unjust, but he does not call it
unholy (*NE* 1159b35-1160a7).[22] What then is the purpose of his religious use of
hosios in *Pol.* II 4?

Before answering this question, I should like to look briefly at the *Republic*'s account of how such crimes will be avoided. Plato writes:

> Unless the rulers command it, it is likely that a younger man will never at-
> tempt to do violence to or strike an older man. And I think he will not dis-
> honor an older man in any other way. For there are two sufficient guardians
> preventing him, fear and shame: shame keeping him from touching his par-
> ents, fear that others will help the one who suffers, some as sons, some as
> brothers, and some as fathers (465a-b; cf. Aristophanes, *Eccl.* 636-643).

This remedy depends on each person actually feeling close familial affection
toward his fellow citizens. But Aristotle believes he has shown that no such
affection will exist among the citizens of the best city of the *Republic*. Instead,
he takes the actions and attitudes of the average Greek as something of a given
(or at the very least it is something that must be taken into consideration). And
experience tells us that wherever there is a community of people, there is the
chance that arguments, abuse, and fights will occur. This is especially true
when men are drinking and where there are men of all age groups.[23] The possibility even exists among members of the same family, but the situation would
be particularly bad in the absence of familial affection.[24]

Now what exactly is Aristotle up to? It is unlikely that he himself accepts
the doctrine of pollution, and yet he thinks that in some way it is problematic.
Since he is discussing affection and the unity of the city, and how Platonic
communism precludes them, he may believe that the communism of women
and children, combined with the ordinary Greek's view of impiety and pollution, somehow leads to a decrease in unity or affection.

According to Aristotle, the "difficulties" mentioned at *Pol.* 1262a25 would
occur in the best city of the *Republic*, even with its communism of women and
children. Moreover, there would be a sense among the people that impious
crimes had been committed without the city knowing it, in which case there
would exist pollution in the city that had not been removed (either through

purification rites, or penalties of exile or death). Adkins (1960, 89) writes that the belief in pollution "is not a belief restricted to tragedy or legend; belief in 'pollution' and its consequences is an everyday feature of life even in Athens in the fifth and fourth centuries: a belief which does not belong merely to some hypersensitive priestly class, but is part of the outlook of the 'ordinary Athenian.'"[25] Aristotle's account depends on this outlook. What effect might it have on a city?

There are, I believe, two factors involved in the "ordinary Athenian's" view of the failure to atone for impious acts that, when combined with the communism of women and children, would not be conducive to a city's unity: fear and shame. These are the same factors Plato thought would prevent such acts, but with these differences: Here the fear is a fear of pollution, and the shame is not shame for an action that may be committed, but for one that might have already been committed.

Fear of the pollution brought about by all types of impious acts will be felt. Men will become suspicious of their neighbors, fearing that by eating at the same table with some person, for example, they might inadvertently become polluted too: The man sitting next to me struck someone last week who might have been his father. Parker (1983, 10) writes: "Religious danger is almost always potentially communal in Greece. . . ." And there is also the fear they will feel for the fate of their city—a city that may be doomed for its failure to atone for an impious act.[26] In the case of shame, the seat of the emotion is in the person who might be polluted. For example, the morning after the night of a drunken brawl with an older man, a young man wakes and reflects on what he may have done, i.e., he may have struck his own father. As a result, he is ashamed to come face-to-face with other men. Oedipus says that he will not be able to look at his parents when he gets to Hades (Sophocles, *Oedipus the King* 1371-74), and a line from Agathon states that "When I consider that I am doing wrong I am ashamed to look my friends in the face" (fr. 22, Nauck).[27]

If my account of *Pol.* 1262a25-32 is correct, then Aristotle's point need not be that these acts will actually pollute the city and, for example, bring about famine. Instead he might be saying that given the views of the average Greek, there will be an overabundance of fear and shame in Plato's best city; and the offspring of fear and shame—distrust and alienation—will greatly preclude unity and affection.[28]

Although it may be impossible to go beyond speculation on this issue, there are two advantages to my position. First, Aristotle's criticism is no longer a marginal point tossed at Plato in passing. Instead it becomes part of the broader project in *Pol.* II 3-4, namely, to show that the communism of women and children does not produce unity (as Plato claims), but actually reduces it.[29] Second, my interpretation is more consistent with what Aristotle says elsewhere about religion.[30]

Aristotle next moves from violent crimes to what might be called sexually perverse acts (*Pol.* 1262a32-40).[31] One might expect him to criticize incest in general, but this is not what he does (i.e., he does not attack all sexual activity between close relatives). The reason could be that incest per se may not have been considered a form of pollution, neither by Greek culture in general, nor by Aristotle in particular.[32] It could also be that Aristotle believed Plato had taken sufficient steps to avoid incest between biological siblings. The *Republic* prohibits sex between those conceived at the same marriage festival (461e). Perhaps it also prohibits more than one "marriage" per couple, so that no two children (putting aside twins, etc.) would have the same set of biological parents and thus no one would ever have sex with a person closer than a half brother or half sister.[33]

In any case, Aristotle focuses on one type of relationship: the homosexual *erastes-eromenos* (lover-beloved) relationship.[34] It is possible that he was motivated in part by an unsympathetic view of Greek homosexuality. At *NE* 1148b15-1149a20, Aristotle adumbrates three unnatural pleasures and the dispositions or states of character that correspond to them. One kind of disposition corresponding to unnatural pleasures includes those that are disease-like and result from habit. Aristotle gives the following examples: pulling one's hair, chewing one's nails, eating dirt, and sex with males. If his attitude toward homosexual relations was as negative as this sounds, this may have been one reason for his focusing on this particular kind of incestuous relationship.[35]

An understanding of Aristotle's criticism requires a brief discussion of the nature of the erastes-eromenos relationship. Dover's excellent work, *Greek Homosexuality* (1989), makes such a discussion possible.

A proper erastes-eromenos relationship is asymmetrical. The erastes (lover) is the older, active, and assertive partner, while the eromenos (beloved) is the younger, passive, and receptive one. In a proper relationship, the same person cannot be both erastes and eromenos. In addition, the eromenos does not share in the physical pleasure that the erastes experiences. (That would be improper.) Whereas the erastes feels *eros*, the eromenos at most feels friendship (*philia*). (See Dover [1989, 16, 52-53, 86-87, 99].) Dover (1989) writes that

an honourable eromenos does not seek or expect sensual pleasure from contact with an erastes, begrudges any contact until the erastes has proved himself worthy of concession, never permits penetration of any orifice in his body, and never assimilates himself to a woman by playing a subordinate role in a position of contact (103; see 106).

What *proper* motivation (i.e., in contrast to the improper motivations of money, physical pleasure, etc.) might a young male have in becoming a partner in such a relationship? The eromenos grants "favors" to the erastes, and in return the erastes improves the eromenos. (Or the erastes improves the eromenos, and in return the eromenos grants "favors" to the erastes.) Thus a proper erastes-eromenos relationship is, in an important respect, an educational relationship. (See Dover [1989], 53, 91, 164, 202.) The favors the eromenos grants may take many forms. Dover (1989, 54, 91) suggests they could include anything from "a kindly smile, [and] a readiness to accompany [the erastes] to watch a race," to kissing, caressing, and sexual intercourse.[36]

Before examining Aristotle's criticism itself, let us look at the passage from the *Republic* that he is commenting on. This passage can be divided into two parts, the first explaining why erotic love and sex should be separated, and the second what law should follow from this.[37]

> [1] Can you think of any pleasure greater or more intense than sexual pleasure (*peri ta Aphrodisia*)? (No I can't, nor a madder one.) Is the naturally right kind of erotic love (*orthos erôs pephuke*) to love (*eran*) the orderly [or well behaved, *kosmou*] and beautiful (*kalou*) in a moderate and cultured way? (Definitely.) And nothing mad or akin to licentiousness must approach the right kind of erotic love? (No, it must not approach it.) Therefore, this pleasure must not approach it, and erastes and boy who love and are loved in the right way must not share in this pleasure? (No, by Zeus, Socrates, this pleasure must not approach erotic love.) [2] So as it seems, you will establish a law in the city that is being founded that an erastes may kiss, be with, and touch his boy as he would a son, for noble reasons, if he persuades him. But otherwise, his intercourse (*homilein*)[38] with anyone he cares for will be such that the relationship will never be thought to go further than these things. If not, he will be subject to blame for being uncultured and lacking in taste [or ignorant or inexperienced about the beautiful, *apeirokalias*] (403a-c).

Plato seems to be prohibiting not only all sexual intercourse between erastes and eromenos, but all sexuality, period. The touching Plato does allow is not the type that usually accompanies this sort of relationship, but that which we would expect between a father and son (cf. the type of touching Phaedo describes to Echecrates at *Phaedo* 89b). As we saw above, normal, proper homosexuality (i.e., what the Greeks tended to consider normal and proper) had a sexual and an educational aspect. Plato, it seems, wants to preserve the latter aspect while obliterating the former.[39] Now why did Plato want to preserve some form of the erastes-eromenos relationship? I think the major reason has to be that, aside from any educational value this sort of relationship has, he thought it was stronger than a familial relationship. And since his aim was the most unity possible, this relationship, if properly tempered, would be a proper means to that end. (See *Phaedrus* 255b and *Symposium* 209c-210c.)

Aristotle criticizes both parts of this passage from the *Republic*, beginning with the second.

> It is also strange that, while making the sons common, only the sexual inter-course (*to suneinai*) of lovers is prevented, but loving (*to eran*) is not for-bidden, nor the other practices, which are most indecent (*aprepestaton*) of all for a father in relation to a son, and a brother in relation to a brother, seeing that loving by itself is (*Pol.* 1262a32-37).

Once again, I think Aristotle's point depends on actual Athenian thought and practice. In Aristotle's view, all Plato has done is prohibit sexual intercourse; but the relationship is still between an erastes and an eromenos, which is qualitatively different from a father-son or brother-brother relationship. The love between them is different: One is eros, the other friendship. Even minus sexual intercourse, there would, given the nature of the Greek male, still arise those "other practices." If the relationship was indeed to remain an erastes-eromenos relationship, then the "other practices, which are most indecent of all for a father in relation to a son," could not be prevented. Dover (1989, 164) writes that "it was taken absolutely for granted that close contact with a beauti-ful, grateful, admiring young male was a virtually irresistible temptation." The erastes, Aristotle seems to think, would not be able to "touch his boy as though he were a son" (*Rep.* 403b) for long. In Xenophon's *Symposium*, we hear of the power the beauty of a young male has to enslave older men (IV 12, 14, 16, 23-4). To kiss such a youth is even worse.

> There is no more terrible fuel of eros [than kissing a beautiful boy]. For it is insatiable and offers some sweet hopes. Because of this I hold that for the one who is able to be in control (*sôphronein*), it is necessary to abstain from kissing those in the bloom of youth (IV 25-26; see IV 28 for the problems involved in touching such a youth).

According to Aristotle, Plato cannot attain what he wants. He hoped for stronger and closer father-son and brother-brother relations among male citi-zens; what he would get is lovers, not fathers, sons, and brothers. There are two great problems with this: (1) some of these lovers might be real (i.e., natural) fathers, sons, and brothers, which is (or is thought to be) most indecent (and if such acts are impious, they will lead to the same problems mentioned earlier); (2) however close an erastes-eromenos relationship might be, it will not lead to more unity in the city, especially if it comes at the expense of familial affection (by replacing father-son and brother-brother relations with erastes-eromenos ones).[40]

Aristotle goes on to criticize the first part of the passage from the *Republic*. "It is also strange that sexual intercourse is prevented for no other reason than the great strength of the pleasure that takes place. But that one [of the partners] is father or son, or that they are brothers, is thought to make no difference" (*Pol.* 1262a37-40). That sexual intercourse is accompanied by great pleasure is not the problem. Placing fathers, sons, and brothers into relationships that will most likely be sexual in nature is.

Politics II 4 (1262a40-b24): The Dilution of Affection

Aristotle's digression completed,[41] we return to the more general issue of the ill effects of communism on affection. This section is meant to "wrap up" the preceding discussion of *Pol.* II 3-4, and to criticize the community of women and children generally.[42]

> On the whole, it is necessary, because of such a law, for that to occur which is the opposite of what correctly established laws will properly cause and of that cause for which Socrates thought it was necessary to arrange in this way the affairs of the women and the children. For we think that friendship is the greatest of the goods for the cities since in this way they [the citizens] would least of all engage in civil strife (*Pol.* 1262b2-9).

We have been given reasons why Socrates' law concerning the arrangement of women and children, instead of holding a city together, keeping it one, actually makes it fractional and more likely to fall apart. (It is important to note that Aristotle—like Plato—regards friendship as an important part of holding the city together. But they differ radically as to the type of friendship that holds the city together.)

Aristotle continues, focusing on Plato's conception of civic friendship.

> Socrates praises most of all the city being one, which is thought to be, and he says is, the work of friendship, just as in the discourses on love [i.e., Plato's *Symposium*] we know that Aristophanes speaks of lovers, because of excess friendship, "desiring to grow together" [191a] and both of them, from being two, to become one (*Pol.* 1262b9-13).

As Plato's Aristophanes is to lovers, Plato's Socrates is to citizens of Kallipolis. Aristophanes wants his lovers to actually become one; Socrates wants the city to actually become one, or at least to become as unified as possible. These similar aims have different consequences. "Now here [i.e., in Aristophanes'

case] both [lovers], or one, necessarily perish, but in the city friendship necessarily becomes watery (*hudarê*) on account of this sort of community, and the
father least of all says 'mine' of his son, or the son of his father" (*Pol.*
1262b14-17). In the former case, the lovers become so unified that either one or
both partners are obliterated. But Plato's city does not become one at all. In
fact, that which (in part) makes the city one (namely friendship) is weakened,
for the reasons we have seen. (Saying friendships become watery is just another
way of saying they become fragmented.)

But there is also a sense in which the two cases have similar consequences.

> For just as a small amount of sweet [wine] mixed with a large amount of
> water makes the combination imperceptible, the relationship to each other
> based on these names [i.e., "father," "son," and "brother"] also occurs in
> this way,[43] it being least of all necessary in a constitution of this sort for a
> father to be concerned with [his sons] as sons, or a son with [his father] as
> father, or [brothers] with each other as brothers (*Pol.* 1262b17-22).

So from the point of view of becoming one, the consequences of Aristophanes'
and Socrates' aims are different. But if we focus on what happens to the partners in the different relationships, the consequences are the same. One or both
of Aristophanes' lovers actually perish. The same is true of each of Socrates'
citizens—not actually, but as father, son, or brother. These relationships become imperceptible. And as a passage from *GC* I 10 illustrates, such watery
relationships are no relationships at all: "a drop of wine is not mixed with ten
thousand measures of water, for its form dissolves, and it changes completely
into water" (328a25-27).

Aristotle concludes by presenting the major reason why Platonic
communism destroys or reduces friendship. "There are two things that most of
all make human beings care (*kêdesthai*) and feel affection (*philein*): That which
is one's own (*to idion*), and that which is dear (*to agapêton*). Neither of these
can belong to those having such a constitution" (*Pol.* 1262b22-24). Nothing is
one's own in Plato's best city, for everything is common. Thus, we could
neither care nor feel affection for anyone in such a city.

A Possible Objection to Aristotle

According to Plato, nearly every citizen in the best city will say "mine" and
"not mine" about the same things and at the same time. They will feel joy and
pain together. And Plato really meant this: They will actually feel close familial
affection toward one another. This, it was claimed, will result in the highest
unity possible. Aristotle replied that this was impossible. In such a city I could
never feel that another is, say, *my* son and thus dear to *me*. Citizens cannot feel

such close affection for so many people. They cannot spread themselves so thin without the affection becoming diluted or fragmented, and thus destroyed.

Much of what Aristotle says, however, is not by itself convincing. Couldn't Plato reply that Aristotle is counting on observations of the average Greek man, but that he has not really shown why such strong affection is impossible, i.e., why it is impossible for a citizen to feel real affection for so many others in the way Plato described? The city of the *Republic* is, after all, radical. Starting from scratch, the guardians will have sent away everyone over the age of ten (*Rep.* 540d-541b). Is it not possible that with the appropriate education, lies, tales, etc., the best city might produce New Men and Women—men and women capable of feeling strong affection for all (or almost all) their fellow citizens? The affection the New Men and Women of the *Republic* feel for all their fellow citizens is arguably not an undetectable drop in the bucket, but distributed in a way that, when combined with affection from every other citizen, adds up to a great deal of affection. If all of this were the case, then many of Aristotle's criticisms could be rejected: that people neglect what is common more; that relationships under a communism of women and children become fractional or diluted; that the recognition of one's real child would cause the actual parent to favor that child over other children; that shame and fear would not preclude impious crimes. All of these depend on what Aristotle knows about humans, but his knowledge is not sufficient, Plato might argue, for it does not include the New Men and Women of the *Republic*.[44]

Aristotle needs to demonstrate, at a more fundamental level, why such close friendship or affection is not possible among many people. I believe Aristotle does show us this, but not in the *Politics*. We need to examine his account of friendship in *NE* VIII-IX (and in his other ethical writings).[45] Such an examination will reveal why, according to Aristotle, it is impossible to feel a high degree of affection for a great number of people.

Friendship and the Proper Number of Friends

In *NE* VIII 2, Aristotle says that three kinds of things are likable: what is good (*agathon*), what is pleasant (*hêdu*), and what is useful (*chrêsimon*) (1155b18-19). Friendship is not only goodwill (*eunous*, i.e., wishing good to others), it is reciprocal goodwill, of which both parties are aware (*NE* 1155b31-1156a5). There are three kinds of friendship, he says, based on the three likable things (*NE* VIII 3, 1156a6-8).[46] The first two are friendship based on utility and friendship based on pleasure. These are the imperfect, or incomplete, types of friendship. They are coincidental (*kata sumbebêkos*, *NE* 1156a16-17): What is liked is not so much the friend's character, but the pleasure or usefulness one receives from a friend. This is not to say Aristotle looks down on these types of friendship. They are classified as friendships *because* they resemble complete friendship. They are, however, easily dissolved, and they can exist among bad people (*NE* 1156a10-b6).

The third type of friendship, complete or perfect (*teleia*) friendship (what I shall be calling character friendship),

> is the friendship of people who are good, and alike in virtue; for they wish goods to each other in the same way *qua* good, and they are good in themselves. And those who wish goods to their friends for the friend's own sake are most of all friends; for they are this way [i.e., friends] because of the friends themselves, and not coincidentally (*NE* 1156b7-11).

Plato's "civic friendship"[47] (i.e., the friendship or affection he believes all fellow citizens in Kallipolis will feel for each other) is not the same as Aristotle's character friendship. Nevertheless, they are both close relationships (at least Plato intends them to be), and thus Aristotle's comments on the latter (concerning how many it is possible to have), I shall argue later, apply to the former as well.[48] So we shall be interested primarily in character friendship, and it is thus necessary to examine in a bit more detail what it involves.

Friendship involves spending time together, and this is especially true of character friendships, where friends wish to live together (*NE* 1171b32).[49] Character friends wish to spend a great deal of time together, both in times of good fortune and bad (*NE* 1155a7-12, 1166a6-8, 1171a21-27). Let us first look at how character friends spend their time together in general (and to what end) and then focus on how a character friend is useful during times of distress and bad fortune.

Living together involves shared activity. Aristotle writes:

> For each person, whatever existence [or being, *to einai*] or that for the sake of which he chooses to live (*to zên*) is, that is what he wishes to do with his friends. Hence some friends drink together and some play dice, while others do gymnastics and go hunting, or study philosophy, each [set of friends] spending their days together engaged in whatever they love most in life. For since they wish to live with their friends, they do those actions and share in those things that they suppose make for living together (*NE* 1172a1-8).

And perhaps most importantly, living together involves shared conversation and thought (*koinônein logôn kai dianoias, NE* 1170b10-14). By spending time together, a good man perceives his friend, thereby perceiving his own being. This is pleasant and good (*NE* 1170a13-b12, 1171b34-35). Such friends also cultivate virtue by living together (*NE* 1155a14-16, 1170a11-13, 1172a10-13).

When a friendship is a close one, as in the case of character friendship, then one friend actually feels the sorrow and joy of the other (at least to the extent that that is possible [*EE* 1240a33-b2]). And only in such a close relationship is a friend able to help another in bad times. "For a friend comforts us by the sight of him and by his words, if he is dexterous (*epidexios*), since he knows (*oide*) our character and what pleases and pains us" (*NE* 1171b2-4). What makes this possible is the knowledge one character friend has of another—a knowledge gained through shared activity. In fact, without such knowledge, a character friendship would not be possible.

We are now better equipped to understand why, according to Aristotle, close friendship or affection is not possible among many people. Too many friends make both the formation and the activity of character friendships impossible. Let us first consider the formation of these friendships.

Character friendships are close. They require that the friends know each other rather intimately, and this takes time. The prospective friends must grow accustomed (*sunêtheias*, *NE* 1156b26) to each other, which requires spending time together. One must discover that the other is likable and trustworthy (*NE* 1156b24-32). Acquiring the necessary knowledge requires comprehension or perception (*NE* 1161b24-27); one must gain experience of the other, or put the other to the test (*empeirian labein, peiran labein*, *NE* 1158a14-15, *EE* 1237b12-13, 1245b25; cf. *NE* 1157a20-25), and form judgments (*EE* 1237b10-12). But all of this is difficult and takes time. Character friendship, in fact, "will not arise among many people, because it is difficult to put many people to the test; for it would be necessary to live with each one" (*EE* 1237b34-36). Aristotle is not saying that a person actually devises some kind of test that the prospective friend must pass; all he is saying is that time will reveal whether a person is good simply, good simply and good to you as well, or not good at all. Time will tell whether a person is a character friend, or one of the other sorts, or no friend at all. For in time one will be able to judge the actions of another: Is he acting like a real friend or not? Why does he like me? etc. Such information is revealed especially in times of misfortune and distress (*EE* 1238a1-20).

Likewise, the activity of character friendship is not possible in relation to many people at the same time (*EE* 1238a8-10). "One cannot live with many people and distribute (*dianemein*) oneself among them" (*NE* 1171a2-4). What Aristotle means, of course, is pleasing another and doing good for him (in the manner proper to a character friendship): A person cannot please or do good for many people (*NE* 1158a13-14).[50] For example, one would have neither the time nor the resources to be properly beneficent to many people in the way one is to a character friend; nor would he be able to console many people who were feeling badly, since this would require an intimate knowledge of each friend and each situation.

There is another sense in which a friend cannot "distribute" himself to many people: "It also becomes difficult to rejoice or to grieve together with many people in a personal [or private] way (*oikeiôs*), for it is likely to happen that one will share in one friend's pleasure and another friend's grief at the same time" (*NE* 1171a6-8; cf. *MM* 1213b13-16). I could easily imagine a situation in which I had two very close friends, one of whom has just become engaged, say, whereas the other has just lost someone very close to him. These would be hard times, finding myself torn between feelings of joy for the one friend and sympathy and suffering over the misfortune of the other. Aristotle's point, however, is probably not that such a situation would be impossible for character friends. More likely he believes that if we actually had many close friends (many more than is appropriate), we would find ourselves in such a situation all the time or at least very often, and that would be unbearable. Moreover, as we have seen, we would neither be able to administer to the needs of the friends who are suffering, nor join in the celebrations of those who are doing well.[51]

So Aristotle concludes that it is impossible to have many character friendships (*NE* 1158a10-11, 1171a8-11). A person should have as many as he is able to live with (*NE* 1171a1-2), and this number will not be that large.

> This would seem to be confirmed in practice. For many people are not friends together in the manner of the friendship of companions, and the celebrated friendships are said to be between two people. But those who have many friends and treat them all as close to them seem to be friends to no one, except in the manner of fellow citizens, and these people are called obsequious. Now it is possible to be a friend to many people in the manner of fellow citizens and not to be obsequious, but a truly decent person. But it is not possible to be a friend to many due to their virtue and for their own sake, and we should be content to find even a few such friends (*NE* 1171a13-20; cf. *EE* 1245b19-25).

Aristotle's results are confirmed by experience, but he did not reach them simply from experience (if by "experience" we mean observations of the way the average Greek acts). Given the nature of humans, it is impossible to know many people intimately, and it is impossible to act as a close friend towards many people. The knowledge and desire to act involved in such a close relationship can be focused only on a very few people.

Character Friendship and Familial Friendship

The arguments against the possibility of having many close friendships were meant by Aristotle to show that one could not be a *character* friend to many people. But Plato in the *Republic*, and Aristotle in criticizing Plato, both have in mind close *familial* affection, *not* character friendship. This is what

Plato claims will give Kallipolis the greatest unity possible. Thus, we cannot assume—it has to be shown—that at least some of Aristotle's arguments count against the formation and activity of familial friendships as well.

The main familial friendships generally and in Kallipolis are parental and sibling friendships or affection.[52] Let us begin with sibling friendships. Aristotle writes:

> Brothers love each other because they have been born of the same parents. For their having the same relation to their parents makes them the same as one another, which is why people speak of the same blood, the same stock, and so on. They are therefore the same thing in a way, in different [individuals]. Being brought up together and being of the same age greatly contribute to friendship, for "two of an age get on well," and those with the same character (*hoi sunêtheis*) are companions. This is why the friendship of brothers is similar to the friendship of companions. . . . What we find in the friendship between brothers is just what we find in the friendship between companions (especially when they are decent, or in general similar), inasmuch as they are more akin to each other and are fond of each other from birth, and inasmuch as those who are from the same parents, nurtured together and educated similarly, are much more similar in character; and the test of time [has been applied in their case] most fully and with the greatest certainty (*NE* 1161b30-1162a1, 1162a9-15; cf. 1161a25-30).

As we can see, the affection or friendship felt between brothers is (or ideally is) very much like character friendship: The friendship is a close one, in large part because of the similarity in character. The formation of such friendships requires, I take it, having the same upbringing, which involves (among other things) spending a lot of time together in close association. And the activities of such friendships are no doubt like those found among character friends. Thus, it is fair to assume that Aristotle's arguments about the impossibility of having many character friends also applies to brothers (or siblings generally in Kallipolis).

We turn now to the "friendship" or affection between parent and child. This is an unequal friendship: The function of each party is different; what they give and get out of the relationship is different. Thus the reasons they feel affection are different, and how much affection they feel is different (*NE* 1158b11-23).

In *NE* VIII 12, where Aristotle discusses parental friendship most fully, he writes:

> Parents are fond of their children because they [i.e., the children] are part of them, while children are fond of their parents because they are something that has come from them. Parents know better what has come from them

than the children know that they are from the parents, and parents regard their children as their own more than the child regards his parents as his own, for what comes from a person belongs to him. . . . The length of time also matters. For parents are fond of their children as soon as they are born, while children become fond of their parents when time has passed and they have acquired comprehension or perception. (From this it is clear why mothers love their children more [than fathers do].) Parents, then, love their children as themselves, for what has come from them is like another self— [another] by being separate (1161b18-29).

Paternal rule is like kingship, since the father (or parent) rules over the children completely, but for the child's own benefit (*Pol.* 1259a10-12, *NE* 1160b24-25). What is the nature of these benefits? Generally, parents confer on their child: existence, nurturing or nourishment, and education or upbringing (*NE* 1161a11-20, 1162a4-10). The parents bring the child into being, as well as give him everything he needs to live (and hopefully live well); and most important, they provide for his education (including his moral education). In the last chapter of the *Nicomachean Ethics*, Aristotle praises common education, but goes on to say:

> Just as in cities laws and characters have force, similarly in the household a father's words and character [or habits] have force, and all the more because of kinship and because of the benefits he confers; for his children are by nature fond of him and ready to obey. Further, education with a view to the individual is better than common education, just as individualized medical treatment is better. For while in general rest and fasting benefit a feverish patient, they may not benefit some individual patient; and the boxing instructor presumably does not recommend the same way of fighting to everyone. So it would seem that treatment is more exactly right when care is particular to individuals since each is more likely to get suitable treatment (1180b3-13).[53]

I think it is clear that however different character friendship and parental friendship are, Aristotle's arguments work equally well against the idea of parental friendship existing among many people. Parents love their children automatically. This comes from the child being a part of them, and thus like themselves. (This suggests something close, in some ways like character friendship.) A child is another self because the parents have imposed their stamp on him. He is the parents' product. The child's love of his parents, however, takes time: He has to see or understand the nature of his parents and the benefits he receives from them. This would involve close contact, living together, forming judgments. Finally, although the activity of a child with respect to his parents is perhaps not important here, the parents' activity with respect to the child is. The care needed to nurture a child, attend to all his or her particular needs, console him or her, and educate him (but not her, for Aristotle) in the way described, requires, Aristotle could argue, the close and focused attention that is found in the traditional Greek household, not a few hundred "fathers" and "mothers" of the sort that would be found in Kallipolis.

The citizens of Kallipolis are supposed to feel close familial affection for one another. They say "mine" and "not mine" at the same time; and when one is doing well or poorly, they all are. Plato says that these are not just words: They would really feel this close (*Rep.* 463c-d). But if so, according to Aristotle they would each require particular knowledge of each particular friend or "family member" (and surely even the Forms would not help—see *NE* I 6). But there would not be enough time in a lifetime to gain such knowledge (considering there would probably be at least a thousand citizens).[54] And even if they could gain such knowledge, there would not be enough time to act like a close friend to all fellow citizens. So despite what Plato says, they would not be friends at all, or they would be friends in name alone.

In the end, it appears Aristotle *is* able to provide a more fundamental defense of his claim that the communism of women and children does not lead to an increase in affection and thus more unity. It is better to have many friendships of varying intensities (see *NE* 1159b29-35), a very few of which are close, than to have a whole city full of "close" friends in name only.

Civic Friendship

We now know what kind of civic friendship (*politikê philia*) Aristotle does *not* advocate; but what are his more positive views about the friendship or affection that *should* be felt among citizens?

It is clear from what has been said that civic friendship cannot be equated with, nor is it a type of, character friendship. It is true that the Greek polis is much smaller than the modern state (and the modern city, for that matter); but no matter how small the population of the polis is, it will be a much larger number than the few character friendships that are possible.[55]

It also seems clear that Aristotle's criticism of Plato, as well as his own account of friendship, rule out any position that sees civic friendship in Aristotle as a relatively intimate relationship involving a close sharing or merging of the lives and goals of the individual citizens.[56] The stronger and more intimate civic friendship is, the more open it is to Aristotle's criticisms of Plato—i.e., that attempting to make civic friendship as close as character or familial friendship would lead to neglect instead of affection, and it would end up fragmented and diluted. So civic friendship must be a much weaker form of friendship than familial or character friendship.

Does this mean that civic friendship must be construed in an extremely narrow way? Annas (1990) thinks so. She rejects the view that there is "a special sort of interest, which is a *friendly* interest on the part of each citizen in every other . . ." (242). Instead she believes that

> civic or political friendship . . . is a friendship between two or a few more people whose shared activities are those of civic involvement, rather than those of religious, family or other involvement. They become friendships, presumably, because they are trying to support the same public measure, ostracize the same politician, and so on (248).

I believe three passages (and there may be others) count strongly against Annas's view. First, at *NE* 1167a22-b3, Aristotle equates civic friendship with concord and says a city possesses concord when its citizens agree. Second, at *EE* 1242a6-9, he ties civic friendship to people coming together to form cities due to a lack of self-sufficiency and to a desire to be in the company of other humans. Finally, at *NE* 1163b32-1164a2, civic friendship is said in part to involve the economic relations between, for example, shoemakers and weavers. These passages show that Aristotle's conception of civic friendship is broader than Annas claims, and broader in two ways. First, civic friendship involves many more people than the two or a few that Annas maintains it involves. Second, it does not simply rise out of an ad hoc political partnership with very narrow political aims. Civic friendship, I hope to show, involves many (ideally all) fellow citizens, with an aim as broad as the good of the city and the citizens in it.

A person, Aristotle says, *can* be a friend to many people in a fellow citizen's way (*NE* 1171a15-17). And civic friendship is a genuine type of friendship. Specifically, it is a type of friendship of utility. "Civic friendship is constituted according to utility" (*to kata chrêsimon*) (*EE* 1242a6-8). "Concord appears to be civic friendship, just as it is said to be. For it is concerned with advantage (*peri ta sumpheronta*) and with what affects our life" (*NE* 1167b2-4). (See also *EE* 1242a5-b26; cf. *EE* 1236a33-34, *MM* 1209b17-19.)

So, at the very least, civic friendship will involve the feeling of goodwill by each citizen for every other (this is qualified somewhat below), where all are aware of this goodwill, and where the source of (and the motivation for) this feeling is the expectation or recognition of the benefits they are receiving or will receive as a result of the relationship they have with their fellow citizens.[57] This does not mean they are indifferent as to whether or not their fellow citizens also receive benefits. The goodwill they feel is genuine, and thus they wish their fellow citizens well.[58]

In the *Eudemian Ethics*, Aristotle writes that civic friendship is not based on superiority, but on equality (1242a9-11, 1242b22, 1242b30-31). This is not to say that there will not be a ruling and a ruled element among the citizens who feel civic friendship for one another. But what is important is that this ruling factor is not natural (*phusikon*, like the rule of a master over a slave) or kingly (*basilikon*), but based on equal rule in turn.[59] So even if we are considering only the correct constitutions, we must set aside as special cases those not based on equality, i.e., on ruling and being ruled in turn. (This would include kingship and most forms of aristocracy).[60] The important point here is that in most cases what fellow citizens feel for one another (as fellow citizens) will be the same.[61]

The most important characteristic of civic friendship is agreement or concord (*homonoia*). Not only is concord a feature of civic friendship, Aristotle says it actually appears to *be* civic friendship (*NE* 1167b2-4, *EE* 1241a32-33). It also seems to be that which is most responsible for holding the city together (*NE* 1155a23-26).

> Concord also appears to be a mark of friendship. Thus it is not merely identity of opinion (*homodoxia*), for this might occur even among people who do not know each other. Nor do we say that people are in concord when they agree about just anything, e.g., those who agree about the heavens (since concord about these things is not a mark of friendship), but we say a city is in concord when [its citizens] agree about what is advantageous, choose the same actions, and act on what they have resolved to do in common. Thus, it is about things to be done that people are in concord . . . (*NE* 1167a22-28).

So civic friendship requires that citizens agree on what the proper conception of justice is, the arrangements concerning the rulers and the ruled, what offices should be elective, with whom the city should make an alliance, etc. (See *Pol.* 1301a35-39, *NE* 1167a28-b2.)[62] Citizens should in general agree on the most basic and most important questions concerning the nature and activities of their constitution. (See *Pol.* 1295b13-33.) Also, citizens must be satisfied that there is justice in the city, not only politically, but economically (i.e., justice in the marketplace). For example, a shoemaker will have to know that he can deal with weavers, doctors, etc., and get a fair price for his goods, paying a fair price for their goods and services (*NE* 1163b32-1164a2; *EE* 1242b21-27). This requires a monetary system, a system of justice, no institutional fraud or corruption, etc. In addition, concord most likely requires that citizens be supportive of the constitution; that is, they must want it to exist, and they should feel benevolence toward it (*Pol.* 1270b21-22, 1320a14-17).

Although Aristotle sometimes speaks of *all* citizens agreeing (e.g., *Pol.* 1320a14-17)—which seems impossible—he more likely means that all the *parts* of the city (especially rich, poor, and middle-class) agree on fundamental constitutional issues (see *Pol.* 1270b20-22; cf. *Pol.* 1294b34-40). Even so, I imagine there are different degrees of concord a city could possess and still meet Aristotle's approval, with the quite unrealistic total unanimity among citizens being at one end of the spectrum. But more likely, there will be at least *some* locking of horns on fundamental political issues.

All friendships of utility—and thus civic friendship—are based on justice (*EE* 1242a11-13).[63] But not all friendships of utility are the same.[64] With respect to justice, there are two kinds of friendship of utility: legal and moral (*nomikê* and *êthikê*). The former is based on an agreement (*kath' homologian*) (e.g., on a contract), the latter is left up to trust, in a way that resembles character friendship. (He says the latter type tends to lead to accusations and is contrary to nature.) (See *EE* 1242b21-1243b14; cf. *NE* 1162b21-1163a23.)

Civic friendship, like the friendships found among cities in an alliance, are *legal* friendships of utility (*EE* 1242b22-25).[65] But even within this category, there are differences in degree. As we shall see, the friendship that exists between cities is an example of a stricter kind of legal friendship. But civic friendship involves more than, or in some sense goes beyond, justice. Citizens should not simply be motivated by contracts or law, Aristotle believes, but also by the goodwill they feel toward their fellow citizens, and, we shall see, by a concern for moral character.

Pol. III 9 contains information crucial to understanding the nature of civic friendship.[66] The city exists not only for the sake of living, but for the sake of living well (1280a31-32). To put it another way, the city does not exist for the same reasons an alliance does, simply to prevent injustice, establish trade agreements, and make military treaties (1280a34-40; cf. *NE* 1157a27-28). It is *necessary* for a city to arrange for these things, but not *sufficient* (1280b29-35).

Aristotle describes the major difference between a city and an alliance in the following way:

> The city does not exist for the sake of an alliance, so that no one suffers injustice, nor for exchange and [commercial] dealings.[67] . . . Those in one city are not concerned that the others [i.e., citizens of another city in the alliance] ought to be of a certain quality or that none of those coming under the treaty [or compact, *tas sunthêkas*] should be unjust or wicked in any way, but only that they should not act unjustly toward one another. But whoever is concerned about good government keeps an eye on political virtue and vice. It is therefore evident that virtue ought to be a care for every city that is truly (i.e., not just nominally) called a city. Otherwise the community becomes an alliance that differs from others [i.e., from alliances whose members are remote allies] only by location. And law becomes a treaty and, as the sophist Lycophron says, a guarantor among one another of the just things, but not that which makes the citizens good and just (1280a34-b12).

Citizens (at any rate, some of them) must be concerned about the moral character of their fellow citizens. (In *Pol.* VII 4, Aristotle writes that citizens must be acquainted with [*gnôrizein*] one another's qualities or worth [1326b14-16].) This makes a city one city (see *Pol.* 1280b13-15), and thus it may be a part of concord (which most of all holds a city together). In fact, concord requires at the very least the following concern for a fellow citizen's moral character: One's beliefs about justice and the virtues generally will affect how one views the nature and activity of the city, (and it is just such opinions that determine whether a city possesses concord). In addition, Aristotle says concord requires that citizens know each other, and he may have had in mind (at least in part) a knowledge of moral character, and thus it may very well be the case that Aristotle included this concern for the moral character of one's fellow citizens in his conception of civic friendship.

Price (1989, 196-204) claims that when Aristotle says a person wishes his fellow citizens well and wants them to be good, this cannot mean that the person wants them to be good because it in some way benefits him. That, Price argues, would make the city no different from an alliance, where we are concerned that the other parties to the alliance are just only to the extent that it benefits us (or because it benefits us). Therefore, Price says, Aristotle must mean that we wish fellow citizens well for their own sake, which makes civic friendship a variety of character friendship: My goals—my happiness—merge with or 'overlap' the happiness of my fellow citizens. Their happiness is a constituent of my happiness, as is true of close character friendships.

But what Price offers us is a false alternative: *Either* the city is like an alliance in the way described, *or* fellow citizens are intimately connected, merging their goals and lives. But a distinct position between these two is possible (and much more plausible): A citizen is interested in the moral character of others not simply because he wants others to fulfill their contracts (though that is part of it). He also wants his fellow citizens to be good (and happy) because he has to live with these people much of the time, engage in activities with them—in the marketplace and at the Assembly, for example. But the source of his interest—and of the goodwill and civic friendship that that entails—is still utility, i.e., the fact that such a situation benefits him.

So far we know that civic friendship involves citizens feeling mutual goodwill, a high degree of concord, a certain connection to legal justice, and (most likely) citizens taking thought for the moral character of their fellow citizens. But we do not yet know how close or intimate this friendship is (if it can be called close or intimate at all). Discovering this, however, at first glance seems problematic. For on the one hand, we know from what was said earlier that civic friendship cannot depend on every citizen having a close relationship with each of his fellow citizens (or even having knowledge of each particular fellow citizen). On the other hand, we know that a citizen (in order to be a "civic friend") must know the political views of his fellow citizens (*NE* 1167a23) as well as their moral character. Is there some way of resolving this apparent contradiction?

As far as I can tell, it can be avoided only if Aristotle maintains that a "civic friend" knows *in general* the moral character of *the citizen body* (e.g., he knows his fellow citizens tend to be just) as well as the general political views of the citizen body (e.g., he knows his fellow citizens tend to be democratic and for the most part believe the city should join in an alliance with Athens).[68] If one concludes that one's fellow citizens tend to be moral and observes that they tend to be in agreement politically, then the relationship one has with a fellow citizen can be described as civic friendship. (No such relationship holds, of course, where one knows that a *particular* fellow citizen is corrupt, say, and/or against the present constitution in some fundamental way.[69]) A citizen need only discover the character and political views of his fellow-citizens generally; a more intimate knowledge is not required. (See Cooper [1990, 233-34n16, 235n18].)

How will citizens come to have the knowledge requisite for civic friendship? Because of friendship, human beings desire to live together (*Pol.* 1280b38-39, *NE* 1155a19-21).[70] This leads them to inhabit one location, intermarry, and partake in such institutions and activities as "clans, festivals, and the pastimes of living together" (*Pol.* 1280b35-38). I believe Cooper (1990, 232-33) is correct in writing that these clans, festivals, etc.

> in turn . . . provide the specific sort of connectedness that, in Greek cities, grounds the interest in and concern by each citizen for the qualities of mind and character of his fellow citizens generally that he has been insisting distinguishes citizenly ties from those provided by contractual agreements for mutual economic advantage. (Cf. Newman [1887, 3:208-9].)

These institutions and activities (in part) provide a citizen with both the knowledge of, and concern for, the ethical qualities of his fellow citizens. In addition to these, political institutions and activities (e.g., meetings in the Assembly) also provide us with this same knowledge and concern, as well as a general knowledge of the (hopefully highly uniform) basic political views of the citizen body.

In chapter 2 I began to present an account of Aristotle's conception of the unity of the city. A city's unity depends on the parts of the city being held together by a certain type of constitution. Related to this, the unity of the city also depends on justice and reciprocal equality. But perhaps equally important, we saw that the unity of a city depends on civic friendship. This more than anything else holds the city together. We are now in a position to complete this account of the unity of the city. Citizens will feel affection for one another due to the mutual benefit they all receive from living together in a city. They agree about what is advantageous for the city: who should rule, how the city should be run, etc.; and to the extent that they care about the common good, they all have one aim.[71] In addition, the affection a citizen feels for his fellow citizens involves a concern for their moral character (and its improvement). For how well one is able to support the city and the constitution, is likely to be loyal and not a traitor, is willing to openly, honestly, and intelligently discuss issues in the Assembly and the Council, is likely to be fair in the marketplace, etc., depends on moral character.

It is the awareness of a common aim and the awareness that everyone accepts it and is working to achieve it (each thereby benefiting himself), manifested in and encouraged by their "living together," that most of all holds a city together.

Plato hoped to hold the best city of the *Republic* together—to give it the most unity possible—by having its citizens feel an intense form of affection for one another. But this, Aristotle has argued, is artificial; and it is bound to fail, for it actually precludes unity—any kind of unity. Aristotle aims for a much lower degree of affection, but it is a level of affection appropriate to adult citizens and to the operation of a city. There are certainly drawbacks to having this type of civic friendship (see *MM* 1211a12-15, *EE* 1242b35-1243a3), but they are not so great that they prevent the city from functioning well—as best a city can. And Aristotle's conception of civic friendship does not preclude other important types of friendship. There will be character friendships, which are necessary for living the best life, and there will be all the different sorts of family friendships (friendships that hold the family together), and so on. All of these are necessary for the best city, and all of them would be missing or deficient in the city of the *Republic*. For the existence of these closer forms of friendship depends in part on the view that the citizens who make up a city are separate entities with their own lives—lives in some ways detached from the city. In trying to eliminate the private, Plato's city must necessarily eliminate our close friendships, all of which are private, i.e., our own.

Notes

1. For a brief discussion of *philia* and related terms, see Cooper (1980, 301-2, 334n4).

2. As I hope will become clear, the fact that Plato uses "most" whereas Aristotle uses "all" is of little or no importance. See note 5 below.

3. See *SE* 166a33ff., 177a33ff., 181b20-24. For examples of "all" used in more than one sense, see *Pol.* 1264b17-22, 1307b35-39, 1332a36-38.

4. It seems that in this particular passage Plato has in mind the guardians alone, not all citizens. It also seems that in *Pol.* II 3-4 Aristotle is aware of this. (See *Pol.* 1262a40-b1.) But on the question of whether Platonic communism is in general intended for all citizens or only the guardians, Aristotle thinks Plato is unclear, and there is something to what he says. (See the appendix.) In any case, Aristotle proceeds as if this close familial affection were intended for all the citizens of the *Republic*.

5. The same ambiguity, or double meaning, could be attributed to the word "most." "Most saying 'mine' and 'not mine'" could mean either "each of however many the most consists of taken individually" or "most (however many of the total that is) taken collectively." So I do not think we can accuse Aristotle of distorting Plato's argument by using "all" instead of "most."

6. On why Aristotle says "the citizen who is doing well or badly," see *Rep.* 463e. This statement makes the affection greater. Not only are all boys of a certain age my sons, their well-being is, in a sense, mine too. Their joys are my joys; their hardships are my hardships. I feel what they feel.

7. *Houtôs*, the sense in which each says "mine," is explained by *hopostos tugchanei ton arithmon ôn*: "what number he happens to be in relation to the number [of citizens]." See Liddell, Scott, and Jones, s.v. *hopostos*. *Ton arithmon* (*Pol.* 1262a3) is an accusative of respect. I take "he"—the one who "becomes" a fraction—to be the citizen doing well or badly. This, however, is by no means clear. But I think "as much as falls to each" from *Pol.* 1261b35 may support my reading. "Each" remains whole but relates to only a fraction of another. (More on this shortly.) The difference between the two readings is one father, say, having 1/nth of a son, rather than a son having 1/nth of a father. This is not a major difference, and Aristotle may very well have had both in mind.

This fractional relation is further explained by *hoion emos ê tou deinos* etc. (*Pol.* 1262a3). On *tou deinos*, see Liddell, Scott, and Jones, s.v. *deina*. The first edition of Liddell and Scott states that *deina* can mean "someone forgotten," i.e., "what's his name." If this is the sense Aristotle has in mind, it may be a joke on Plato.

8. Bornemann translates *tou deinos* with "der X. oder des Y. oder des Z." Although this is not a literal translation, it is basically Aristotle's meaning. Plato would object that each citizen would say "my son *and* A's son and B's son, etc." rather than "my son *or* A's son, etc." But in the end, this is precisely what Aristotle claims is impossible.

9. We need not take this too literally. I do not believe Aristotle thought the affection one felt could be measured precisely and represented by a fraction—that in a communistic city of 1125 citizens, say, each young male will feel towards me exactly 1/1125th what a son feels towards his father normally. Aristotle's point is simply that the communism of women and children leads to a decrease in, or fragmentation of, affection.

10. The *Republic* has eliminated the bases for all the different kinds of affection, aiming instead at the closest affection for all. If this fails (as Aristotle claims it must) there will therefore be (practically) no affection in the city. Cooper (1990, 233n15) writes: "The misguided attempt to achieve this [i.e., close familial affection in all for all] *both* does away with true family ties *and* makes impossible true civic friendship. All you get is a watered-down family friendship."

11. The recognition of one's relatives (often when it is too late) is an important part of Greek tragedy. See *Poetics* 11, 14, 16, and Schütrumpf (1991, 2: 181).

12. See *Rhet.* 1360a30-37.

13. Family resemblance was, for Aristotle, a serious object of scientific investigation. (See *GA* IV 3.)

14. See *HA* 586a12-14.

15. The *tous de hekousious* is omitted in some manuscripts.

16. Aubonnet (1960, 138n9) writes: "Aristote dans la Politique, comme un Hellène ayant les sentiments religieux de son temps et de sa race, ne néglige pas la considération de *to hosion*." (He cites *Pol.* 1335b25 for support of his view, but he is not correct: see note 18 below.) Cf. Parker (1983, 124).

Saxonhouse (1985, 15n2) claims "Aristotle is not so concerned with the watering down of love as he is with the consequences of that watering down, that is, impiety." I will argue for the opposite interpretation: Aristotle is concerned with impiety *only* to the extent that it undermines political unity.

17. Newman is citing J. Bernays, *Theophrastos' Schrift über Frömmigkeit* (Berlin, 1866). Additional support for this view of the Peripatetics may be found in Theophrastus, *Characters* XVI, on superstition and the superstitious man (*deisidaimonia, deisidaimôn*). Not only does he criticize what many at the time would regard as superstitious (e.g., anxiety caused by a pole-cat crossing one's path), he also lampoons so-called omens and being overly concerned about purification and pollution. See Ussher (1960, 135-57).

On Aristotle's exoteric lectures and writings—those open or available to the public, and thus most likely presented with the views of the public in mind—see Guthrie (1981, 53-59). On dialectic, see especially *Top.* I 2.

18. *NE* 1096a16 says that holiness requires that we honor truth (i.e., that there are no Forms) above our friends (i.e., the Platonists). *Pol.* 1335b25 states that with respect to abortion, what is holy is defined by reference to perception and life. The former sounds more like justice than piety; the latter may be religious, but is not necessarily so. Cf. *NE* 1166b5 and *Pol.* 1253a36, where Aristotle connects "unholiness" or "impiety" (*anosiourgôn, anosiôtaton*) with the lack of virtue.

19. Dover (1974, 246-54) and Adkins (1960, 132-33). See also Burkert (1985, 269-70) and Connor (1988, 162-64, 170).

20. For an excellent discussion of this topic, see Parker (1983). See also Burkert (1985, 75-84). Aristotle does not actually use the term *miasma* in the present passage.

21. See Adkins (1960, 102-8, 136-38), and Sorabji (1980, 289, 292-93).

22. Although I claim Aristotle does not accept the traditional view of pollution, I do not mean to suggest that he did not, for example, regard the killing of one's father (even involuntarily) as especially horrible—more horrible than killing a stranger. To this extent his views are similar to the traditional religious ones.

23. See Antiphon[?], *Tetrologies* III 3.2, 4.2, where the topic is a youth who has killed an older man in a drunken brawl. See also Aristotle[?], *Probl.* III 2 and 27, where drunkenness is tied to poor judgment and troublemaking.

24. For some examples of improper actions committed against family members, see Dover (1974, 187, 248, 273-75).

25. On pollution and its expiation, see Parker (1983, passim) and Adkins (1960, 86-87, 92).

26. On fear, pollution, and the ill effects of pollution on man, see Parker (1983, 318). With particular reference to the family, see pp. 122-24, 133, 205. On pollution and its danger to the city, see pp. 128-30, 257-80, and consider the following passage from Herodotus: "After the Pelasgians killed the [Athenian] children and women [i.e., the Athenian women they kidnapped, and the children these women gave birth to in captivity], the land did not bear fruit, and the [Pelasgian] women and flocks did not give birth as they did before" (VI 139). Cf. Sophocles, *Oedipus the King* 23-30, 97-102, 236-43. Ussher (1960, 145) writes that "the basis of purificatory rites could be fear more than the desire to be 'clean.'"

27. Translation from Dover (1974, 236). Cf. Xenophon, *Mem.* II 2.14. On the general misery and separation from others that follows being polluted, see Euripides, *Heracles* 1279-1302.

28. Is Aristotle's criticism of Plato successful? An affirmative answer depends on an affirmative response to two other questions: (1) Does Aristotle, in the other parts of *Pol.* II 3-4, succeed in showing that the communism of women and children is improper and/or impractical? (2) Is it wrong for Plato to present his picture of the best city without concern for what the average Athenian might think? I think the answer to the first question is yes (and this will, I hope, be clear by the end of this chapter). However, I think the answer to the second question is no (but to defend this would take us beyond the scope of this chapter).

29. This may be a dialectical argument not for the sake of knowledge itself, but as an aid (*sunergon*) in answering some other question (see *Top.* 104b3-4, 9-11), in this case, Is the communism of women and children a proper political arrangement? This kind of argument from *endoxa* (here, that certain acts are impious and cause pollution) does not *establish* the claim that a communism of women and children is improper, but supports it.

30. Aristotle does not believe in the traditional Greek gods. He uses the term "god" (*theos*) to refer to natural things like the Prime mover and celestial bodies (*Met.* XII and *Phys.* VIII). He even calls the elements gods (*GC* 333b21). The truths of philosophy, however, will not be grasped or believed by everyone. The opinions of most people will accord with the traditional views of the gods. (See *DC* 270b5-9, 284a2-23, *Meteor.* 339b19-30, *Met.* 1000a5-20, *Pol.* 1314b38, *Poet.* 1460b35, and Connor [1988, 171-85]. Connor writes: "Popular attitudes were likely to be strongly in favor of the view that

sacrifices and worship of the gods were essential for civic well-being" [184].) These traditional beliefs are important:

> From the most ancient times it has been handed down to posterity, in the form of a myth, that these [i.e., the unmoved movers, or perhaps the stars, see Ross (1924, 2:395)] are gods and that the divine embraces [or encloses] the whole of nature. *The rest has been added later in mythical form with a view to the persuasion of the many and with a view to its legal and beneficial use (Met.* 1074b1-5).

The city's attitude toward religion must take into consideration—be shaped by—what most men actually think, even if their beliefs are not true. Fortunately, the city can use these beliefs to its own advantage. This is why even in the best city of the *Politics* there are priests and temples devoted not to the Prime Mover, but to the traditional gods. (See *Pol.* 1328b12-13, 1329a27-34, 1330a13, 1331a24, 1335b15, 1336b16; cf. 1299a17, 1322b18-22.) Usually these beliefs can be used to improve civic virtue and habituate citizens toward proper action. In the case of impiety, however, I do not think Aristotle is concerned with the promotion of inherently proper civic behavior. His point is that it must be recognized that citizens will have strong beliefs about what is and is not unholy, and the failure to construct a constitution accordingly could undermine the city's unity.

    31. Aristotle does not call the latter impious. But since he treats these acts immediately following violent impious crimes and he lists some of them together—"outrages, erotic passion, and homicide"—at *Pol.* 1262b30, it is perhaps safe to assume that he classified them both as impious acts or crimes. But see the following note.

    With the upcoming criticism in mind, Bornemann (1923, 137) writes: "Auch hier finden wir wieder schwere Mißverständnisse und keine Spur von Fähigkeit, sich in Platons Vorstellungen hineinzudenken." As I hope will become clear, the misunderstanding is Bornemann's.

    32. See Adkins (1960, 110n17). But cf. Plato's *Laws* 838a-839b and Parker (1983, 95-98, 220-21). Parker writes that

> it is difficult to prove that incest is a "pollution." Here, too, problems arise about the definition of the term. Incest is nowhere spoken of as *miasma*, and it does not seem that it was even formally illegal at Athens, much less that the offender was publicly expelled to purify the state. In one passage in Euripides, however, Oedipus is said, immediately after a reference to his marriage, to be "polluting the city," and the idea of religious danger is present in the common claim that such a match is *anosios*, offensive to the gods. The incestuous could be socially isolated without exile, by exclusion from sacrificial communities and marriage exchanges. It was believed in later antiquity that Cimon incurred actual ostracism because of his relations with [his sister] Elpinice. . . . On an imaginative level, an analogy is clearly felt between incest . . . and the worst pollutions. In the myth of Oedipus, it is associated with parricide. . . . Incest, particularly that between generations, is, therefore, one of the supreme horrors of the imagination that define by contrast the norms of ordered existence. It lies in a sense beyond pollution, because it is beyond purification (97-98).

    33. MacDowell (1986, 86), describing Athenian marriage law, writes:

A woman could not be legally married to a direct ascendant or descendant (grandfather, father, son, grandson), nor to her brother or half-brother by the same mother. But she could be married to her half-brother by the same father, to her brother by adoption, or to her uncle, cousin, or more distant relative, or of course to a man who was not a relative at all.

34. Both *erastês* and *erômenos* are related to the word *erôs* (sexual love or desire). However, the English terms "lover" and "beloved" do not really capture their meaning. I shall therefore simply use the transliteration of these two words throughout. (Their meaning will become clearer shortly.)

35. For a brief discussion of Aristotle's views on homosexuality, see Dover (1989, 168-70). Dover believes this *Nicomachean Ethics* passage refers to *passive* homosexuality only, and he may be right. On the apparent connection or moral similarity between homosexuality and incest, see Plato, *Laws* 838a-839b.

36. According to Dover, to be proper the intercourse had to be intercrural (1989, 98-99), but this is controversial. See Cantarella (1992).

37. In the translation that follows, I have removed the "he said's" and "I said's," and placed Glaucon's responses in parentheses.

38. As with the English "intercourse," this term has both a sexual and nonsexual meaning.

39. See Dover (1989, 156-59) on the broad use of "erastes" in Plato.

40. Aristotle states that erastes-eromenos relationships are prone to quarrels and often fade (*NE* 1164a2-12, 1157a5-10). Halperin (1990, 30) writes that "Not only is sex in classical Athens not intrinsically relational or collaborative in character; it is, further, a deeply polarizing experience: it effectively divides, classifies, and distributes its participants into distinct and radically opposed categories." There may have been on the reader's mind something tying this criticism to the last one (on violent impious crimes), namely, fights over eromenos. See Dover (1989, 42, 56-57, 189-90n12).

41. The digression began back at *Pol.* II 3, 1262a14.

42. Aristotle begins this section with what might very well be a joke of sorts. "The women and children being common would seem to be more useful to the farmers than to the guardians. For there will be less friendship where children and women are common, but the ruled should be this way with a view to obeying and not attempting political change [or innovation (*neôterizein*)]" (*Pol.* 1262a40-b3). Aristotle is most likely saying something like the following: "Plato, if you're going to have a political institution that diminishes affection, you should at least use it to your own (city's) advantage. Since you don't want innovation (see *Rep.* 424b-e, 545c-d), wouldn't it be best to keep members of the lower class at each other's throats, thus making them less troublesome?" Though somewhat speculative, this interpretation is more desirable than that of Susemihl and Hicks (1894, 230): "The strength of this [the lower] class excites Aristotle's fears."

43. In what follows (1262b20), I accept the manuscripts over Dreizehnter's (1970) changes.

44. Objections to Aristotle along these lines are found in Susemihl and Hicks (1894, 222, 228), Bornemann (1923, 132-41), Mulgan (1977, 39), and Saunders (1992,

106-7). Simpson (1991, 111-12) considers this objection and replies that since the communism of women and children is part of the education of the guardians (he cites *Rep.* 464a8-b7, 464c5-e2), "the guardians on whom it is to be imposed must be taken to have, before the imposition, all the passions and weaknesses of ordinary human beings." Thus, he claims, Aristotle is justified in attacking Plato in the way he does. But Plato's defenders could respond in any of the following ways: (1) The primary purpose of the communism of women and children is more the increased unity of the city through an increase in affection than it is the upbringing of the guardians (see the passages cited by Simpson). (2) Even if it is to be counted as part of their education, it is not the only (or even the primary) part, so there is no reason to believe the young New Men and Women of the *Republic* will have the same passions and weaknesses as the other Greeks simply because they have not experienced communism's contribution to their education. (3) Most important, there will in fact be no period "before this imposition" of the communism of women and children (aside from the period before the initial founding of the city). The guardians (or citizens) of the *Republic* are (or will be) born into it. They will reap the benefits of it, Plato could argue, from the very beginning. So Aristotle is still in need of a fuller defense of his criticism of Plato.

45. While investigating Aristotle's criticisms of Plato's *Republic*, I was pleased to have discovered that Stalley (1991, 193) also regards the discussion of why it is impossible for a person to have many character friends as relevant to Aristotle's criticism of Plato. However, he does not (understandably, in the context of a brief article on the whole of *Pol.* II 1-5) develop this idea fully.

46. These three can be further divided into equal and unequal types. See *EE* 1239a1-4, 1242b2-4, *MM* 1210a23-24, *NE* 1158a33-36, 1158b11-28.

47. Plato never uses the term civic friendship (*politikē philia*) in the *Republic*.

48. One could argue in defense of Plato (with some plausibility) that these close relationships of familial affection are to exist only among the guardians, and that the friendship found among the iron and bronze citizens will be a friendship of utility. But see note 4 above.

49. "Living together" does not refer to living in the same house but to living one's life with another person, sharing activities, etc.

50. It is impossible in the case of character friendship. In the case of friendships of utility or pleasure, doing good to many is possible, but not advisable, as it is a hindrance to living well (*NE* 1158a16-18, 1170b23-29).

51. We have so far been talking about the difficulties involved in *one* person trying to have many character friends, and we saw that he could not acquire the requisite knowledge of so many people, nor engage in the appropriate activities in relation to so many people. But what is even worse is the fact that these many people "must be friends of one another, if they are all to spend their days together; and this is hard work when there are many people" (*NE* 1171a4-6).

52. Aristotle speaks of parent-child and father-son relations, and the relationship between brothers (never sisters). But given the role of women in the running of Kallipolis, I shall speak in terms of parental and sibling relationships.

"Marriages" are temporary in Kallipolis, thus it is better to view males and females of roughly the same age as siblings. (Treating them as spouses would not significantly alter the arguments against Plato.)

53. In *Pol.* VIII 1, Aristotle condemns private education and praises a common form of education. However contradictory this may sound, I take it that Aristotle has something like the following in mind: It should not be up to each individual to decide what kind of education (especially moral education) their child should receive. The state should set goals, curriculum, standards, etc., but the job of *implementing* them is in part that of the parent (and especially the father). He will best know the individual needs of his own child.

54. Note the similarities with the last chapter, where a lack of knowledge on the part of the guardians prevented the city from being self-sufficient.

55. Irwin (1990) recognizes that civic friendship seems to be a kind of friendship of utility, but he argues that because this does not show what is intrinsically good about political activity, we must turn to character friendship in describing the relationship between fellow citizens. (See Price [1989, 193-205] for a similar position.) This is hopeless, he notes (recognizing that one cannot have many friends in the manner of character friendship), but not a waste of time. He thus extends civic friendship to include aspects of character friendship (e.g., we will regard fellow citizens as other selves). But this move is highly speculative, and quite dubious in light of Aristotle's criticism of Plato in *Pol.* II 3-4. (More on this below.)

56. I have in mind Irwin (1990) (see the previous note, and the criticism of his views in Striker [1990]), Price (1989, 193-205), and Cooper (1990, 236-41). Price (1989, 205n36) writes: "Although Cooper and I attach different labels to civic friendship (he of 'utility', I of 'virtue'), we are still trying to make sense . . . of what is in substance the same conception." On Cooper's position, see Miller (1995, 202-3, 208-9). I should also point out that in contrast to Irwin, Price, and (perhaps) Cooper, I do not regard civic friendship as a constituent (or at least not an important constituent) of happiness. Civic friendship is in my view an instrumental good. (See Striker [1990].) This will become clearer below.

57. This suggests that the deviant regimes (i.e., tyranny, oligarchy, and democracy) will not be characterized by civic friendship in any essential or complete way, at least not between the rulers and the ruled. For in these regimes the rulers do not care about the common good; they are only concerned about their own advantage. Rulers neither care about, nor act to benefit, the ruled. (See *Pol.* III 7. Cf. *Pol.* 1309a33-35, *NE* 1161a32-34.)

58. Though I cannot get into the issue here, I should at least point out that I agree with Cooper's argument for the view that in friendships of utility and pleasure as well as in character friendships, one wishes one's friend well for the friend's sake. See Cooper (1980, 308-15).

59. See *EE* 1242b27-30. I think it is clear that Aristotle is not referring to proportional equality, in the sense that, for example, a proportion can be found in the relationship between a king and his subjects that equalizes their relationship. See the next two notes.

60. See *NE* VIII 10-11. Consider the following example: In a kingship, there will be the normal civic friendship among the ruled, but what they feel for their king, and what their king feels for them, cannot be called civic friendship, for it is an unequal friendship, namely, paternal friendship (*NE* 1160b24-27, 1161a10-15). See Cooper (1990, 238), though I do not believe that in an aristocracy the friendship between the nobles or the virtuous and the other citizens is properly—in most cases—civic friendship.

61. Even where equal citizens are ruled and rule in turn, there will be some differences in how the ruled treat the rulers. But these differences are minor. See *Pol.* 1259b7-8.

62. Perhaps the most important aspect of concord is agreement about the system of rule. "There is concord when the same choice [has been made] concerning who is to rule and who is to be ruled. . . . Concord is civic friendship" (*EE* 1241a30-33).

63. Justice and friendship, Aristotle says, are either the same or not very far apart. (See *NE* 1159b25-1160a8, *EE* 1234b18-31.)

64. There are different types or degrees of friendship of utility. For example, the affection you feel for the doctor you have gone to for the past ten years will be greater than the affection you feel for your average fellow citizen, though both are friendships of utility. And as we shall see, civic friendship will be greater than the friendship characteristic of alliances. Etc.

65. This is yet another reason why we should *not* consider civic friendship to be a form of character friendship.

66. The importance of *Pol.* III 9 was brought to my attention by Cooper (1990).

67. I translate *tēn chrēsin pros allêlous* with "[commercial] dealings." I believe it refers to other commercial transactions besides exchange. (Cf. *Rep.* 369b-c.)

68. Cf. Cooper (1990, 233-34n16, 235n18). Aristotle speaks of a citizen's goodwill for the city, and of cities in an alliance being friends (*Pol.* 1320a14-17, *NE* 1157a25-28), so it is not implausible that he thought civic friendship involved a person feeling friendship for the citizen body as a whole.

69. Disagreements among citizens are of course bound to occur. (See Yack [1993, 118-27].) Such disagreements may be what the author of the *Magna Moralia* has in mind when he writes that the friendship between a citizen and a foreigner is more solid than that between fellow citizens (1211a6-16).

70. This is not civic friendship, but a more general form of friendship that arises among people of the same race or among human beings generally.

71. On the need for concord and why it is essential for the unity of any political community, consider the following passage from Lincoln's famous speech delivered June 16, 1858, at Springfield, Illinois:

> We are now far into the fifth year, since a policy was initiated, with the avowed object, and confident promise, of putting an end to slavery agitation. Under the operation of that policy, that agitation has not only, not ceased, but has constantly augmented. In my opinion, it will not cease, until a crisis shall have been reached, and passed. "A house divided against itself cannot stand." I believe this government cannot endure, permanently half slave and half free. I do not expect the Union to be dissolved—I do not expect the house to

fall—but I do expect it will cease to be divided. It will become all one thing, or all the other. Either the opponents of slavery, will arrest the further spread of it, and place it where the public mind shall rest in the belief that it is in course of ultimate extinction; or its advocates will push it forward, till it shall become alike lawful in all the States, old as well as new—North as well as South.

For an excellent ancient example of the terrible effects of a lack of concord, see Thucydides III 69-85.

Chapter Five

Unity and Property

> Always the greater part of the painful fighting is the work of my [Achilles']
> hands; but when the time comes to distribute the booty, yours [Agamem-
> non's] is far the greater reward, and I with some small thing yet dear to me
> go back to my ships when I am weary with fighting. Now I am returning to
> Phthia, since it is much better to go home again with my curved ships, and
> I am minded no longer to stay here dishonored and pile up your wealth and
> luxury.
>
> Homer, *Iliad* I 165-71 (trans. Richard Lattimore)

> From each according to his ability, to each according to his need!
> Karl Marx, *Critique of the Gotha Programme*

Politics II 5 (1262b37-1263a8): Introduction

It remains to investigate Aristotle's criticisms of the communism of property as a means to the aim of the *Republic*, as well as his own views on property.[1]

At the beginning of *Pol.* II 5, Aristotle writes: "Following these things,[2] it
is [left] to investigate property (*ktêseôs*),[3] the way it ought to be arranged for
those who intend to live under the best constitution, whether property is to be
common or not common" (1262b37-40). Now although the communism of
property is connected to the earlier discussion of the communism of women and
children,

> someone could in fact investigate it apart from the laws laid down concern-
> ing children and women; I mean that with respect to the matters connected
> with property, even if those [i.e., women and children] are separate [i.e., not

held in common], which is the way it is now for all,[4] [someone could inves-
tigate] whether it is better for both possessions and their use to be common[5]
(1262b40-1263a3).

And indeed, Aristotle examines the communism of property separately (though
he does mention some important connections between the community of property and issues raised in earlier chapters).[6]

Aristotle considers three possible arrangements concerning property and its
use: (1) property is private, use is common; (2) property is common, use is private; (3) property is common, use is common. Why doesn't Aristotle consider
private property, private use? Miller (1991, 237) claims he omits this option
because "He is not defending a system of unqualified privatization." But this is
not the reason. As we come to find out, one friend giving something to another,
or in fact any act of generosity, falls under private property, common use (view
1). For instance, this horse is mine, but I share it with—i.e., make it common
to—my friend. Thus, this fourth "option"—private property, private use—is no
option at all, for it would be a property arrangement that systematically ruled
out any kind of giving or sharing of one's private property.[7]

Aristotle gives examples of each of these arrangements:

> For example, [1] the plots of land are separate [i.e., private], while the crops
> are brought into the common [store] (*to koinon*) and consumed [in common],
> just as some of the nations do. Or [2] the opposite: the land is common and
> farmed in common, while the crops are divided with a view to private use
> (some of the barbarians are said to share in common in this way, too). Or
> [3], the plots of land and the crops are common (*Pol.* 1263a3-8).[8]

It is extremely important to keep in mind that the three examples he mentions
are just examples. So although Aristotle's position will fall under one of the
three possibilities—we later find he accepts view 1—that position may be quite
different from the example he gives here.[9]

The question for Aristotle now becomes: Which is better, a private property
arrangement (view 1) or a system where property is common (view 2 or 3)?
Aristotle presents several arguments against the latter and for the former.[10]

Politics II 5 (1263a8-21): Impracticality and Injustice

Aristotle begins his criticism of the communism of property with what has
been (correctly) called a "standing difficulty of communist schemes" (Susemihl
and Hicks [1894, 233]). (I divide the passage into two sections for convenient
reference.)

[a] Now if the farmers were others (*heterôn*) [than the citizens],[11] the manner [in which property would be managed (cf. *Pol.* 1262b37-38)] would be different (*allos*) and easier; but if they [i.e., the citizens who are farmers] do the hard work by themselves, the matters connected with possessions will lead to greater discontent (*duskolias*). [b] For in fact, when in the enjoyment [of things] (*apolausesi*)[12] and in work they are not equal, but unequal, accusations will necessarily be raised against those enjoying or taking many things while laboring little by those taking less while laboring more (*Pol.* 1263a8-15).

In a sense, the point Aristotle is making is quite straightforward. When property is held in common, some people will do more work than others but will receive only the same as those who do less (which is less than those who work hard deserve). But there are two questions that must still be answered: First, is Aristotle criticizing the communism of property here simply because he thinks it is impractical (i.e., it leads to greater discontent, which is inimical to the city's unity), or, beyond this, does he hold that such a system is unjust as well? Second, by whom, exactly, and toward whom, is this discontent felt?

The first question can be answered by considering some key texts from outside of *Pol.* II 5. The first is from *NE* V 3:

> For if [the people involved] are not equal, they will not [justly] possess equal things, but from this comes fights and accusations (*egklêmata*) whenever things are distributed and equals possess unequal [shares] or unequals equal [shares]. Further, this is clear from what is according to worth (*kat' axian*). For everyone agrees that the just in distributions must be according to some worth; what is worthy, however, not everyone calls the same thing (1131a22-27; see *Pol.* 1280a16-22).

In *Pol.* V 3 he writes:

> It is also clear what honor is capable of and how it is the cause of factional conflict (*staseôs*). For being dishonored and seeing others honored, [people] engage in factional conflict. These [i.e., the honoring and dishonoring] happen unjustly whenever certain persons are honored or dishonored contrary to their worth (*para tên axian*), and justly whenever according to their worth (1302b10-14).

Justice, of course, involves equals getting equal shares (of whatever is being distributed), and unequals unequal shares. (This idea runs throughout *NE* V.) Whether one deserves equal or unequal shares depends on each person's worth (and what is held to be worthy). A lack of justice (or an apparent lack of justice) leads to quarrels and accusations (the latter being mentioned in the passage from *Pol.* II 5 now under consideration). One is honored or dishonored justly depending on whether he gets what he deserves (that is, what he is worth), and unjust (that is, contrary to worth) dishonor can lead to factional conflict. (See *Pol.* 1266b28-31 and 1267a37-b9.)

So it seems Aristotle is making the following two points: First, having some people work more and yet receive the same as others (who work less) leads to discontent (and possibly to conflicts). This occurs where property is common. Second, this situation is unjust, for unequals are clearly receiving equal rewards. (True, equality and inequality depend on what is thought worthy and unworthy, but in this context, the standard must be the ability to work well and/or hard.[13])This second point implies that Aristotle's criticism of the *Republic* is less consequentialist than some have thought. Aristotle's position is not simply that it is unworkable, but that it is also in some ways unjust. (Cf. Charles [1988, 200].)

Now to the second question. Of the two sections of our passage, [a] is the more problematic since the Greek is especially ambiguous. I believe, however, that the standard interpretation (which is represented in the above translation of 1263a8-15) is correct, at least to the following extent: I take [a] to be saying that Plato makes the farmers and other workers (i.e., the iron and bronze class) citizens, whereas the situation would be easier (i.e., the city would be easier to govern) if the laborers were not citizens but slaves, serfs, or the like. (Part [b] then describes why this is so, i.e., it describes what grave problem will be likely to arise if the workers are citizens.) This reading seems to be confirmed by what Aristotle writes elsewhere: When describing his own best city, he says that the farmers should be slaves or barbarians, not citizens (*Pol.* 1329a25-26, 1330a25-30). Similarly, he says that the fighting class and the farming element should be different, i.e., they should be citizens and noncitizens respectively (*Pol.* 1329a40-b2, 1329b36-38). Finally, in his view slaves (unlike citizens) are in no position (or are much less likely) to complain about unfair or unjust treatment.[14]

As for [b], the question I want to answer is this: whom does Aristotle have in mind? i.e., by whom, exactly, is this discontent felt? Or to put it another way, who will be making these accusations, and against whom? In answering this question, I part company with the standard reading of this passage.

The standard interpretation of *Pol.* 1263a8-15 maintains that Aristotle is referring to the iron and bronze citizens of the *Republic* on the one hand, and the gold and silver citizens on the other. In this view, Aristotle believes that because the iron and bronze citizens do the hard work—the farming, smithing, etc.—whereas the gold and silver do not, and because the gold and silver men enjoy or have more than the iron and bronze, the iron and bronze citizens will feel resentment toward the gold and silver citizens (whereas if the work proper to the iron and bronze class were done by slaves, there would not be this problem, or there would be less of a problem).[15] If this interpretation were correct, Aristotle should be criticized, on the grounds that the gold and silver citizens do not have or enjoy more than the other citizens. The gold citizens (the rulers) in a sense rule against their will (*Rep.* 517c-520d); and although the gold and silver citizens receive a "wage" for necessities from the iron and bronze men (*Rep.* 416d-e, 463b), in general they own nothing, whereas the iron and bronze citizens do in some sense (however limited, regulated, controlled) have (or have contact with) possessions and property (*Rep.* 369e-371e, 373b-d, 416e-417a).[16]

There is, however, a more plausible interpretation of *Pol.* 1263a8-15. Aristotle most likely has in mind not all citizens, but the iron and bronze citizens alone. Under a system where property is common, all workers would have the same claim to things (i.e., they would share the property in common), yet some workers would have done more work than others. As a result, the workers who have done more work would get less than they deserve, whereas others would get more, and this, Aristotle claims, is likely to lead to accusations and discontent among the workers, as we have seen. So unless Aristotle had little or no grasp of Plato's *Republic* (a view I see no reason to accept[17]), my interpretation of *Pol.* 1263a8-15 is surely the better of the two.

One interesting and important implication of my interpretation is this: We can conclude that, at least with respect to the distribution of property, Aristotle is most emphatically not a proto-Marxist (nor Marx an Aristotelian) as is sometimes claimed. (See Nussbaum [1988 and 1990].) For it is clear that Aristotle would reject Marx's famous line from the *Critique of the Gotha Programme*: "From each according to his ability, to each according to his needs!"

Aristotle concludes that "In general, living together and sharing in common in all human matters is difficult, and most of all in these sorts of things [i.e., concerning property]" (*Pol.* 1263a15-16). This conclusion is justified from the earlier criticisms of the communism of women and children (some of which apply to property as well [see *Pol.* 1261b23-1262a1]), from the criticism just discussed, and from some easily observable facts (of which he gives two examples).[18] First, "the communities of fellow travelers reveal this, for most of them are at odds from clashes (*proskrouontes*) with one another over pedestrian and small things" (*Pol.* 1263a17-19; cf. 1303b17-18). It is unclear whether this is an example of a "human matter" generally, or of the sharing of property in particular. But in any case, fellow travelers have some kind of community, and thus, to that extent they share something in common (see *NE* 1159b26-32). For example, they may buy some wine, bread, and onions to share during their trip (and they might even have common funds). But they could very well come to blows over who drank more wine, had more bread, and so on. "And further, we clash most of all with those of the servants we use most for ordinary tasks" (*Pol.* 1263a19-21). Humans are such that they do not even need to share property for disputes to arise. Simply occupying the same space, working together on the same job, and the like, will do it. Where there is human association, the potential for conflict exists. An increase in association (as in communism) will produce an increase in the potential for conflict.

Politics II 5 (1263a27-29):
Communism and Productivity

Aristotle also claims the communism of property will reduce productivity. He writes that "dividing the care [of possessions], they will not make accusations against each other, but rather they will improve, as each attends to his own" (*Pol.* 1263a27-29).[19] Now what did Aristotle have in mind? He probably meant for us to think back to *Pol.* II 3, where he was criticizing the communism of women and children: At *Pol.* 1261b32-40, he said that people who share things in common neglect those things because they think others are taking care of them. This applies to property as well. (See *Pol.* 1261b23 and *Oec.* 1344b34-1345a1.) If I own one acre of land, I shall most likely see to it that it is cared for and productive. But if I am one of 1000 citizens who share 1000 acres in common, each acre is likely to be much less cared for and much less productive. That is Aristotle's point. Not only does private property avoid the accusations and conflicts discussed above, it also improves the citizens' well-being by making them more productive.[20]

Politics II 5 (1263b15-29): Communism and Crime

We have seen problems not only with the full-fledged communism of property, but with a very limited sharing of life and property as well. Aristotle believes these problems are enough to rule out the communism of property. But one could argue that although communism might lead to some problems, it would avoid others. This in fact is the reputation communism has come to have. Aristotle writes:

> This sort of lawmaking [that is, communism] is fair of face (*euprosôpos*)[21] and might be thought humane (*philanthrôpos*), for he who hears it receives it gladly, thinking that some marvelous affection will come to be in all for all, especially when someone charges that the evils now belonging to constitutions come about through property not being common. I mean lawsuits against one another concerning contracts, trials for perjury, and flattery of the rich (*Pol.* 1263b15-22).[22]

Aristotle has in mind the view that perjury, contractual disputes, flattery of the rich, theft, and the like, can exist only when property is held privately and unequally, and thus that the communism of property should be instituted, since it will eliminate such injustices.[23] He replies: "none of these things come about through lack of community, but through wickedness (mochthêrian) since we see those who possess in common and have much in common at odds more than those holding property separately" (Pol. 1263b22-25). Communism is not the answer, Aristotle says, because the cause of these injustices is not private property, but wickedness. The evidence for this is that although we might see people who hold property privately committing these acts, we see these same actions (or some of them) committed by those sharing property in common—in fact, we see those sharing property in common committing even more of these actions.[24]

But if the communism of property is not the answer to these problems, what is? We cannot simply say private property, since these acts can also be committed when property is private. To find Aristotle's answer we must go to Pol. II 7, where he criticizes the view (held by Phaleas and others) that property should be leveled.[25]

It is claimed that the communism of property—or leveling property generally—could cure the injustices associated with property since all (or nearly all) crimes are committed in order to acquire the necessities of life. By ensuring that everyone has the necessities of life (and equal amounts of these), there would be no reason to commit unjust and shameful actions—neither to get what one wants, nor because of envy. Aristotle rejects this claim, for he challenges the idea that crimes are committed simply in order to acquire necessities.[26] There are in fact, he says, three reasons why crimes are committed (Pol. 1267a2-9): (1) to acquire the necessities of life (e.g., food, clothing); (2) to satisfy desires for things that are beyond what is necessary (e.g., a drunk who wants more wine than is good for him, a man who kills from a desire for revenge); (3) to experience painless pleasures (e.g., through tyranny or philosophy).[27] There are three remedies corresponding to the three causes of crime (Pol. 1267a9-12): (1) a minimum amount of property and work, for whoever has these would not need to commit crimes in order to possess the necessities of life; (2) moderation, for a moderate man does not desire more than is proper;[28] (3) the philosophical disposition or life, for this is the greatest of the painless pleasures, and the man with a truly philosophical disposition will not commit crimes. (See Pol. 1323a24-34.)

Aristotle claims that in fact the greater crimes are not committed to acquire necessities, but for one of the other two reasons: "They commit the greatest injustices because of excesses, not because of necessary things. For example, [people] are not tyrants in order to avoid being cold. . . . So it is with a view to minor injustices alone that Phaleas' type of constitution is of assistance" (Pol. 1267a12-17). The solution to the problem of what to do about crime is not the leveling of property, but the improvement of character through education (*Pol.* 1266b28-31). It is better for desirable ends to be achieved by the improvement of a citizen's character through education than by trying to compel citizens to act in certain ways through the control or abolition of their property. As we shall see, this is a central part of Aristotle's view of property.

Politics II 5 (1263a40-b14):
Communism Destroys Certain Pleasures and Virtues

In addition to the above problems, Aristotle argues, the communism of property would diminish or destroy certain kinds of pleasure: "Further, with regard to pleasure, too, it makes an immense difference to consider something one's own. For it is not without reason that each person has affection for himself; this is natural" (*Pol.* 1263a40-b1).[29] Aristotle is claiming that because we naturally feel affection for ourselves, what is our own is therefore pleasant to us. But it is unclear how or even if this inference is justified. A passage from *Rhet.* I 11, however, sheds some light on the point he is trying to make.

> Since that which is according to nature is pleasant, and things related to each other are according to nature, all related and similar things are pleasant [to each other], for the most part; for example, man [is pleasant] to man, a horse to a horse, a young person to a young person. . . . And since everything that is similar and related to oneself is pleasant, and each man himself is this way most of all in relation to himself, everyone necessarily is a lover of self, more or less. For all such things belong most of all [to one's relationship] to oneself. And since everyone is a lover of self, one's things (*ta hautōn*) are necessarily pleasant to everyone [individually], for example, deeds and words (*erga kai logous*) (1371b12-23).

It does not seem (at first) that we have made progress, for Aristotle at the end of this passage claims that a man finds his own things pleasant because every man is a lover of self. But this is precisely what we are attempting to explain. Thus, we have to see if there is in Aristotle some way of justifying this inference. A way has been suggested by Miller (1991, 239):

> True self-love is embodied in persons who act according to their own rational judgment (cf. *Eth. Nic.* 9.8.1168b34-1169a3). True self-love thus requires that persons be able to act according to their own judgment, and the existence of private property provides them the sphere in which they can do so.

So the important part of Aristotle's argument (for our purposes), given Miller's suggestion and the above passages from the *Politics* and the *Rhetoric*, may very well be something like the following: (1) Every man (or good man) has affection for himself. (2) The natural (including what is naturally beloved) is pleasant. (3) Therefore, every man finds himself pleasant. (4) For a man to find himself pleasant is to find all those things that essentially make up his self pleasant (his character, his own rational judgment, his actions that follow his judgment, his "deeds and words"). (5) By extension, a man will find pleasant whatever makes his self possible—for instance, whatever makes possible voluntary action according to his own rational judgment. (6) Having his own things (including private property) makes possible such judgment and action. (7) Therefore, a man finds his own things pleasant.

The important premises are (4) through (6). Although Aristotle does not state them explicitly, they are necessary if the argument is to be complete. Aristotle could have argued that because a person's own things are related to him (naturally or properly), he derives pleasure from them. But he says more than this: A man gets pleasure from things that are his own because he has affection for himself, and this requires that Aristotle hold something like premises (4) through (6).

The important move—from the point of view of the critique of Plato's *Republic*—is Aristotle's argument that because there are pleasures in things being one's own, and since nothing is one's own in a communistic system, it follows that where property is common, the pleasures connected with things being one's own are destroyed or diminished. But Aristotle's point may be deeper; and, if true, it would reveal a greater problem with Plato's best city (or communism generally). For if it is true that having things that are our own is a condition of acting according to our own judgment, then communism not only destroys the pleasures associated with things being our own and the affection we feel for ourselves, it would also seem to undercut our autonomy (that is, our ability to act according to our own judgment).

Still on the subject of pleasures, Aristotle writes that "doing favors for and helping friends, guests, or mates is most pleasant, and this happens when property is private. These things do not occur for those who make the city too much of a unity" (*Pol.* 1263b5-8). This argument is similar to the previous one: (1) Generosity[30] (like every virtue) is pleasant (see *NE* 1120a25-31). (2) Generosity requires private property (see *NE* 1178a28-29, *Pol.* 1265a34-38). (3) Private property does not exist where property is common. (4) Therefore, generosity cannot exist where property is common. (5) Therefore, where property is common, men will be deprived of the pleasures connected with generosity.

As is clear from this argument (it is actually stated in premise [4]), not only is the pleasure connected with generosity destroyed, so must the virtue itself be destroyed. The communism of property will destroy the work or function of "generosity concerning possessions, for no one will be known to be generous or do generous actions, since the work of generosity is in the use of possessions" (*Pol.* 1263b11-14).[31] Again, Aristotle's argument has something like the following form: (1) Generosity (or the activity of generosity) requires private possessions. (2) Where property is common there are no private possessions. (3) Therefore, where property is common there is no generosity (or no generous activity involving possessions). If generosity is destroyed, then the function or work of generosity (that is, the result of people acting generously), is destroyed.[32]

The soundness of this argument, however, depends on the truth of premise (1) (as did the soundness of the previous argument depend on the truth of premise [2]). But can this premise be defended? Irwin (1987, 51-52) claims that it cannot:

> My own generosity may be properly expressed through my role in collective actions; it does not seem to need resources under my exclusive control. Even if we think the practice of generosity requires me to be free to dispose of some resources on my own initiative, it does not follow that the resources must be under my exclusive control. The state might loan them to me, and allow me to dispose of them as I please within certain limits and in certain circumstances; such an arrangement would leave ample room for the exercise of generosity.
>
> We might argue that this is not real generosity, if the virtuous person's action does not cost him anything, and that it does not cost him anything unless he gives from his exclusive possessions. But this objection seems to overlook the virtuous person's attachment to the common good. He will regard the distribution of his friend's resources as a cost to himself, because he regards his friend's resources as his own; and he will take the same view of the community's resources. We might object that such identification of one's own interest with the interests of others is impossible or undesirable; but Aristotle should not be easily persuaded by any such objection, since it would undermine his whole account of friendship. Perfectly genuine generosity seems to be quite possible without private property; and to this extent private property seems unnecessary for anything of distinctive value.

There are two major problems with Irwin's argument: First, as we have seen, according to Aristotle we will not, and indeed cannot, attend to common things very well—in fact we tend to neglect them. For this and other reasons, I cannot feel for the community's resources what I feel for myself and my own things—I cannot truly regard the former as my own. (See *Pol.* 1261b23, 1261b32-40, 1263a27-29, 1263a40-b1.) Second, I might regard the distribution of a close friend's (or family member's) resources as a cost to me since, in a sense, the goods of such friends are common. But I do not have the same relationship with the community, and thus neither do I view the community's resources in this way.[33] Thus, I shall indeed need my own resources if I am to act generously.[34]

It is true, Aristotle would say, that the communism of property could eliminate some problems (for example, if all property were common, there would not be disputes in court over debts owed). This would amount to a handful of small advantages, however, compared to a host of problems—all the problems we have seen so far. "But it is just to speak not only of how many evils they will be deprived of when they have [property] in common, but also how many goods. This life appears to be wholly impossible" (*Pol.* 1263b27-29). The communism of property makes life impossible, whatever problems it might eliminate. But a system of private property (if arranged correctly) is wholly desirable, whatever problems might remain.

Politics II 5 (1263a21-40): The Proper Attitude toward Property

What is a properly arranged system of private property? What system of property did Aristotle advocate?

> But the way that exists now [concerning property], if adorned with character (*êthesi*) and an order of correct laws, would differ not a little [from the communism of property]. For it would have what is good from both. By "from both" I mean from possessions being common in some way, but private generally (*Pol.* 1263a22-27).

Property is to remain private, but with some adornments that give it the advantages of common, as well as of private, property. (What these adornments are will be seen later.)

Although private property is clearly better than the communism of property, property should still be common in some sense: Its use should be common. "It will be through virtue that, with regard to use, 'the things of friends are common' (as the proverb says)" (*Pol.* 1263a29-30). It turns out that this is not necessarily a radical suggestion. "Even now this is the way it is in some cities in outline, so it is not impossible; and in finely managed [cities] most of all some of these things exist, while some of them could come to be" (*Pol.* 1263a30-33).

Property will be common in use through virtue (whatever that means), but Aristotle also says "It is . . . evident that it is better for possessions to be private, but to make them common in use. That they [the citizens] become such [as to use possessions in common], this is a special function of the legislator" (*Pol.* 1263a37-40).

There are several questions that must be answered if we are fully to understand Aristotle's views on property. First, what exactly does he mean when he says property should be used in common? Next, how private is private property? That is to say, surely there will be some common or public property—but how much? And to what extent, if any, will private property be limited and regulated? Finally, how does the legislator make citizens become such as to use their property in common and properly? Does he simply pass laws to that effect? We shall proceed to answer these questions, beginning with *Pol.* II 5, but going beyond it.

Let us start by looking at the common use of private property. The first thing to be said is that there seem to be degrees of common use. "For each owning possessions privately, some things are made useful to his friends, while some are used in common" (*Pol.* 1263a33-35). Aristotle is talking here about two different kinds of sharing, both of which constitute making what I own common in use: some things I share in common with certain people (for instance, close friends), but not with others; and some things I make available to everybody (or all citizens). Each citizen will share some (but not all?) of his possessions with his close friends (but not with everyone), whereas some other possessions he will make available to all his fellow citizens. The level of friendship will determine just how common one makes his possessions. Aristotle gives an example. "In Lakedaimon, they use each other's slaves as their own, so to speak, as well as horses and dogs, and provisions for travel, if they need any, from the farms throughout the territory" (*Pol.* 1263a35-37).[35] This passage becomes a bit clearer if read in conjunction with Xenophon's discussion of these arrangements in *LC* VI 3-5.

> And [Lycurgus] made it such that, if someone needed to, he could also use someone else's servants. And he joined together a community of hunting dogs, so that those needing them invite [the owner] to go to the hunt, but if he does not himself have the time to go, he sends [the dogs] with pleasure. And they use horses in the same manner. For one who is sick or is in need of a carriage or wishes to go somewhere quickly, if he sees there is a horse somewhere, after taking it and using it properly, he restores it. . . . Wherever people coming late from the hunt are in need of provisions, if they did not happen to have packed anything, he also set it down that in that case those who possess something should leave behind the [leftover] prepared food, while those in need break the seals, take however much they need, return [what is left over], sealing [the container]. Accordingly, in this way, giving shares to each other, those who have little partake in all of the things in the region whenever they need something.

In Xenophon's account, property is private, and there is a concern (and respect) for private property. However, if someone owns something, but is not using it (or will not be using it, in the case of leftovers), he should make these things available to his fellow citizens. As a consequence, those who otherwise would not be able to have the advantages of a horse, or take part in a hunt, or the like, are able to. Aristotle would seem to agree with this much, given that he chose these practices to illustrate a system he praises.

So far we know that common use involves sharing servants, horses, hunting dogs, and food for the hunt. What else? In his summary of the practices of the Lakedaimonians, Aristotle mentions provisions for travel from the farms throughout the territory. Although this may simply be a generalization from the principle wherein leftovers should be placed in containers, Aristotle most likely found this general principle an important part of what it is to share one's property in common. For example, writing in the *Athenian Constitution*, he[36] says that Cimon "maintained many of his fellow demesmen, for any man of Laciadae who wished could go to him each day and obtain his basic needs, and all his land was unfenced, so that anyone that wished could enjoy the fruit" (27.3, trans. P. J. Rhodes).[37] One way a citizen (especially a wealthy citizen) can make the use of his private property common is to give needy citizens access to his lands. This is one important reason (others being the financing of the military and the arts) that Aristotle regarded wealthy citizens as a crucial part of the city. (See *Pol.* 1283a16-19, 1328b10, 1328b22-23, 1329a19, 1341a28.)[38]

Not only does generosity give the needy access to things from which they would otherwise be excluded, it also helps hold the city together. In *Pol.* VI 5, Aristotle says: "It is also fine to imitate the practices of the Tarentines.[39] For these people, making their possessions common in use for the poor, maintain the goodwill (*eunoun*) of the multitude" (*Pol.* 1320b9-11). As was mentioned before, Aristotle thinks there should be different degrees of what one is willing to make useful to others. Perhaps he believes servants and hunting dogs will be more limited (that is, I might share them, but not with just anyone), whereas the practice with horses or with food in the fields will be more communal.

One important question concerning common use remains: Is such use voluntary, or is it to be enforced by law?[40] Nussbaum (1990, 23) claims it is the latter. She writes: "Aristotle's insistence on common use—that it ought to be possible for a needy person to help herself to your crops, without penalty and with goodwill—shows that in any case he did not defend private ownership in the form in which most contemporary thought defends it." In a note to this passage, she continues: "One might fruitfully compare to this housing policies that have been adopted in some socialist and social-democratic countries, giving the homeless certain rights toward unoccupied or luxury housing" (249n86). I believe Nussbaum has failed to grasp the essential nature of Aristotle's view that property should be private generally, but common in use. First, according to Aristotle, when I make my property (which is private) common in use, I do so from virtue and in the manner of friends. This certainly sounds voluntary.[41]

Second, Nussbaum's conception of common use seems to conflict with Aristotle's conception of what it is for property to be private. In *Rhet.* I 5, he writes that something is one's own (*oikeia*) "whenever the [ability] to dispose (*apallotriôsai*) is with oneself. And I mean by 'dispose' 'giving' and 'selling.'" Generally, being wealthy is in the using more than in the possessing" (1361a21-24; see Miller [1991, 229-30]). If property is really to be private (which I take to be close to the above sense of "one's own"), then the power to dispose of property—even to allow others to use it in common—must be with the owner. If I possess something, but do not control its use, then it is not really mine. So Aristotle is not advocating (at least not for the best city) the transferring of certain of my property "rights" to my more needy fellow citizens.

Then what exactly will "private property, common use" be like in practice? To give an example, a needy person will be able to help himself to my lands if I (not because compelled to do so by law, but voluntarily) unfence my lands (à la Cimon) so that needy people can enjoy the fruit. But in addition, the lawmakers may (or must) do something to encourage owners to make their property common in use in certain ways. For instance, perhaps they could see to it that containers are set up to hold leftovers in the field; and, they could establish laws that make it impossible for the owner of a horse, say, to bring to court someone who uses his horse in the way described by Xenophon. And as we shall see later, there is much more that the legislator must do to make citizens have generous characters.

I have argued that Aristotle's conception of making one's property common in use is not meant as a legal restriction or limitation on the use of one's property. Such use is voluntary. Still, does Aristotle allow for no limitations on private property? And how much of the property in a city should be privately owned? Let us look at the latter question first.

While describing the best city in *Pol.* VII 10, Aristotle says it is necessary to discuss the distribution of land. As a prelude to such a discussion, he mentions the following four points: (1) Possessions should not be common, but should "become common in use, in a friendly way (*philikôs*[42])" (1329b41-1330a2). (2) No citizen should lack sustenance (1330a2). (3) "Concerning common meals (*peri sussitiôn*) all agree it is useful for them to belong to well-equipped cities. (The reason for which we agree will be stated later.[43]) All citizens should share in these, but it is not easy for the poor to contribute the set [or required] amount from their private funds and manage the rest of their household" (1330a3-8). (4) Expenses relating to the gods are, or should be, common to the whole city (1330a8-9). Given these four points, how should property be arranged for those who wish to live under the best constitution?[44]

Aristotle believes that in order for a city to count as the best one could hope for, it would have to have (among other things) the following division of territory (*Pol.* 1330a9-15). Taking it for granted that the city will also have territory on which government buildings (e.g., the Assembly) will stand, and putting that land aside, the following describes how the rest of the land would be distributed: part of the land should be common, and part should be private. These two parts should further be divided such that part of the public land houses common dining halls and produces crops (and funds?) that enable all to participate in them, while another part supports public service to the gods; the private land will be divided such that every citizen will possess land near the city as well as land near the frontier.[45] There is, however, no indication of how exactly the city's land is to be divided. So we cannot assume, as Nussbaum (1990, 204) does, that "fully half the city's land will be held in common."[46]

Let us focus now on public or common land. There should be land to house government buildings, temples, and common dining halls, as well as land that produces enough income to support their maintenance (or part of that maintenance), perhaps including pay for those involved in their upkeep. (See Harrison [1968, 1:234-5], *Pol.* VII 12.) City-owned land would produce crops and livestock (and perhaps precious metals[47]) to support these institutions. The city might also rely on other surplus revenues. (Although they are sometimes warranted, Aristotle does not emphasize taxes, especially not in his discussion of the best city. I shall have more to say on this later.)

In *Pol.* II 9, Aristotle criticizes the Spartan system of common meals, and praises the Cretan.

> The law concerning common meals . . . has not been framed finely by the one first establishing it. For the gathering should rather exist from common funds, as in Crete. But among the Spartans everyone must pay, even some who are exceedingly poor and not able to afford this expense. . . . It is not easy for the very poor to participate in [the common meals], but this is the definition of the constitution among them, passed down from their fathers: the one who is not able to pay this fee is not to participate in it [i.e., in the constitution] (1271a26-37).

In *Pol.* II 10, he again comments on the superiority of the Cretan system of common meals.

> In Crete [the common meals are set up] in a more common manner, for from all the crops and livestock that come from the public lands and from tribute (*phoroi*) (which the subjects pay), one part is set aside for the gods and for common liturgies, and another for the common meals, so that everyone (women, children, and men) is maintained from the common funds (1272a16-21).[48]

The land on which the common dining halls stand is common land, and the common crops and funds (which come from the common lands) should

ideally pay for the common meals of everyone.[49] But how extensive are common meals? It seems quite clear (unless Aristotle was intending something entirely radical) that they took place every day and once a day. It was the main
meal of the day (*to deipnon*), which took place at sunset.[50] But who was allowed to attend? Despite what Aristotle says, it seems the Cretan common
meals were attended by adult male citizens (including the poor), and boys.
Women, Dosiadas tells us, were in charge of the meals, but they did not seem to
partake of them. There is no mention of daughters anywhere.[51] It is of course
possible that Aristotle read into, or embellished, earlier accounts of the Cretan
common meals a bit (much like Plato in the *Laws* may have), so that men,
women, and children all receive meals there. In any case, it is fairly clear that
Aristotle himself supports the inclusion of women in common meals.

So, Aristotle wants the city to see to it that each citizen (and his family)
receives at least the main meal of the day. In this way the basic sustenance of
every citizen is guaranteed.[52]

Generally, the possessions of citizens are private, and citizens possess land
privately, though they can (and should) make some of their land and possessions common in use in the ways indicated. But what limitations (with respect
to amount and/or use) should there be on private property? Aristotle obviously
advocated limits on the criminal use of property—e.g., if I aimed to be selling
pure wine, it would be illegal for me to water it down. But what else? A good
place to begin is with the first two necessary offices. Aristotle writes: "First . . .
is the superintendence concerning the market (*epimeleia . . . hê peri tên
agoran*), for which there should be some office overseeing agreements and orderliness" (*Pol.* 1321b12-14).[53] It is clear that their main functions are to see
that everyone involved is honest and sticks to their agreements and contracts,
and that orderliness (*eukosmia*) is maintained.[54] But Harrison (1968, 2:25)
writes that (in Athens) market supervisors also fixed certain prices. In *AC* 51
(which describes this office), although the emphasis is on preventing fraud and
dishonesty, there is some mention of price fixing, especially the price of wheat.
Rhodes (1993, 577-79), commenting on *AC* 51, writes that "Athens had relied
on imported corn [i.e., wheat] to supplement the local crop, . . . and to ensure
that the citizens should be fed the state was led to take a special interest in the
corn trade. . . . [T]he importers were not free to sell their corn wherever they
could get the highest price for it." It is unclear whether Aristotle advocates any
of this, but he may have. In general, though, the "limits" on private property
implied by this necessary office are not that intrusive, i.e., putting aside fraud
and such, a citizen is left at liberty to use his property as he wishes. In fact, one
main concern is the protection of private property against fraudulent activity in
the marketplace. (Cf. Barnes [1990, 258].)

The second necessary office is town management (*astunomia*). This office
has three functions (*Pol.* 1321b18-27): (i) superintendence of private and public

property in town, with a view to ensuring orderliness; (ii) superintendence of the preservation and repair of decaying buildings and roads; (iii) the prevention of boundary disputes.[55] Barnes (1990, 288-89) complains:

> What exactly is the function of these officials with regard to private houses? May they do no more than (1) order the repair of dilapidated property when it endangers neighbors or passers-by? (E.g., may they instruct me to mend my tottering chimneys? . . .) Or may they also (2) regulate any alterations or repairs I make to my house which could in any way affect third parties? (E.g., may they require me to paint the external woodwork in a seemly colour? . . .) Or may they further (3) determine how I deal with the internal affairs of my house, affairs which affect only its occupants? (E.g., may they prohibit me from installing an electric socket in my bathroom? . . .) These three possibilities mark out, for the modern thinker, three different attitudes to political liberty. Possibility (1) illustrates an old fashioned liberalism. Possibility (3) illustrates a new fashioned paternalism. Any theorist who interests himself in political liberty must take a stand on these questions. Aristotle takes no stand.

Is this fair? True, there is much that is unclear. But can we say nothing? Must we conclude that Aristotle takes no stand? I am not so sure. Function (iii) clearly applies only to what is happening outside of the house. As for functions (i) and (ii), the *Athenian Constitution* might shed some light: "They prevent buildings which encroach on the streets, balconies which extend over the streets, overhead drainpipes which discharge into the street, and window-shutters which open into the street" (50.2, trans. P. J. Rhodes). Much of this no doubt describes function (ii). As for function (i), Aristotle may have seen it implied in the other two functions: seeing to it that my drainpipes do not throw water on to passers-by, and preventing boundary disputes, do promote public orderliness (see Harrison [1968, 2:25]).

In any event, of the three possibilities mentioned by Barnes above, although it is unclear whether Aristotle would have embraced (1) or (2), we have no reason to believe he would have accepted (3). Given the nature of the first necessary office, the description of the second necessary office in the *Athenian Constitution*, and even the discussions of this second office in Plato's *Laws* (see note 55), there is no indication of the sort of paternalism described by Barnes. Again, the limits on property are not so intrusive. So to this extent at least, Aristotle does takes a stand.

Thus, the superintendence of market and property does not imply any (great) restrictions or limitations on private property. But we cannot conclude that Aristotle had anything like a laissez-faire view, for he seems to have advocated a ceiling on how much one may own, primarily in order to avoid what he thought were harmful disparities of wealth and poverty (especially, it should be added, in nonideal situations).[56] In fact, given his distinction between the natural and unnatural acquisition of wealth (*Pol.* I 8-11), even in the best city he would have put a limit on the acquisition of wealth. (See Miller [1991, 235-37].) But it is unclear what kind of restriction this implies: Would wealthy citizens be taxed? Would any money they made (over the ceiling) be handed over to the city?[57] In the best city, some citizens would be wealthy, but they would most likely not be able to acquire an "unnatural" amount of wealth because citizens are forbidden the merchant's or businessman's life. (Of course, this is itself a restriction on property.[58])

Although there may be limits to wealth, Aristotle is obviously not eliminating the wealthy altogether. In fact they are a crucial part of the city. Moreover, he opposes as unjust the confiscation of the property of the wealthy, at least the confiscation of anything below the limit on wealth (see *Pol.* 1281a15-21, 1309a14-19, 1318a25-26, 1320a5-10). Sustenance for the needy (as we have seen) should ideally come from generosity and the common lands, not (in the best circumstances, at least) from the redistribution of wealth (but see *Pol.* 1320b2-4).

Is this to say Aristotle is against taxes? Some passages certainly imply that the wealthy will be taxed, for political (and especially military) functions.[59] But at other places he writes as if taxes are certainly not ideal. (See *Pol.* 1309a14-26, VI 5; Newman [1887, 4:399-400, 532].) This apparent discrepancy can be resolved in the following way: Aristotle believes that in the very best situation, funds from common lands, the generosity of citizens, and so forth, will cover all the city's expenses. But this is not very usual or likely. Normally, even in the best of cities, funds from common lands will cover much of the city's expenses, but some wealth from the richest citizens will be needed to cover what is left (especially if a lot of money is required for the military). To acquire such funds, taxes would be employed.

It seems that in most cases, Aristotle believed that a citizen's property (any that did not go above a certain ceiling on wealth) was that citizen's to use, so long as he did not use it fraudulently and as long as there were enough funds for the city to function properly. If there were not, the wealthy citizens would have to give some of their wealth to the city to meet these needs. (See Miller [1991, 240-45].)

Politics II 5 (1263b36-40): Education and Property

I have claimed that when Aristotle advocates making property common in use, what he has in mind is a voluntary use of property. But then what did Aristotle mean when he said: "That they [the citizens] become such [as to use possessions in common], this is a special function of the legislator" (*Pol.*

1263a39-40)? The only cogent answer is: public education. "Being a multitude
. . . , it is necessary to make [the city] common and one through education"
(*Pol.* 1263b36-37). The legislator must make laws controlling the upbringing of
children,[60] both through making laws that will properly influence them and
through the establishment of a system of public education. As a result, when
they become adult citizens, they will (generally) be of such character that they
will freely share their property with friends and fellow citizens in the ways
described.[61]

As we have seen, Aristotle is critical of any substantial deprivation of freedom. However, because of the fundamental importance of education in the life
of the city, he advocates a coercive view of the education of the young. In *Pol.*
VIII 1, he claims that the legislator must make the education of the young his
object above all (1337a11-14). He goes on to say that:

> Since there is one end (*telos*) for the city as a whole, it is clear that educa-
> tion must necessarily be one and the same for all, and that the superin-
> tendence of it should be common and not private (this latter being the man-
> ner in which each individual at present superintends his own offspring pri-
> vately and teaches them whatever private learning he thinks best). For
> common things the training too should be made common.[62] At the same
> time, one ought not even consider (*nomizein*) that some citizen is of himself
> [or belongs to himself, *autou*], but that all [citizens] are of the city [or be-
> long to the city, *tês poleôs*], for each is a part of the city (1337a21-32).[63]

It is better to have a lack of freedom in one important area—in the education of
one's children—than in the whole of one's life. This education may be coercive,
Aristotle would argue, but it makes possible independent and responsible citizens who do not have to be coerced in every aspect of their lives. And it is better to have a city made up of good citizens, each of whom is free to use his
property as he likes, but who will most likely use it properly (because of his
character, feelings of friendship, and so on), than laws strictly regulating the
use of private property, or abolishing it altogether. (See *Pol.* 1266b24-31; cf.
Plato, *Laws* 740a.) This is what Aristotle has in mind when he writes (*contra*
Plato): "It is strange for one who intends to introduce education and who thinks
that through this the city will be excellent, to suppose that it can be set right by
these sorts of things, but not by habits [or character, *ethesi*], philosophy, and
laws" (*Pol.* 1263b37-40). Platonic civic unity is achieved through "these sorts
of things," namely, laws forcing humans to share property in common, to treat
each other as "brothers," and the like. Aristotelian unity, however, is achieved
through character, philosophy, and laws—i.e., through laws and public education that properly shape the character of the citizens, but then allow these citizens to act independently, control their own property, and so on.[64]

As we saw in chapter 3, Aristotle believes that to live well we need external goods, as well as goods of the body and goods of the soul. Many of these external goods are best described as property. But the need for external goods does not by itself tell us in what way property must be arranged. What we have discovered in this chapter is that given Aristotle's conception of the unity of the city—which stresses the importance of independence, justice, and moral character—citizens ought to possess property privately.

Notes

1. Aristotle first objects to certain aspects of the communism of property, turns to his own view of how property should be arranged, and then presents some other criticisms of the communism of property. I wish to devote a lot of space to Aristotle's own views on property, and believe the clearest presentation is achieved by first presenting all of his criticisms of the communism of property together.

2. *Echomenon toutôn*, possibly "connected with these things." The discussion in *Pol.* II 5 is connected to that in *Pol.* II 1-4.

3. *Ktêsis* can mean "acquisition" or "possession"; in the plural it can also mean "property" (Liddell, Scott, and Jones, s.v.). In Aristotle, however, it is sometimes best to translate even the singular as "property." *Ousia* is also used as "property." On the ambiguity in property terminology at this time, see Harrison (1968, 1:200-201).

4. The way it is now for all the Greeks (not for the Libyans mentioned at *Pol.* 1262a19-21, for instance).

5. Lord (1984, 60) and others (see the apparatus in Dreizhenter [1970, 29]) mark a lacuna here. This is probably not necessary (nor is the replacement of *kai* ["and"] with *ê* ["or"], which is found in the text of Ross [1957, 32]). However, it is at least implied that we follow the line "whether it is better for both possessions and their use to be common" with one of the following: (1) "or for their to be some other system"; (2) "or not"; (3) "or whether it is better to have one common and one private."

6. The communism of property was most likely a part of the intellectual climate at this time. By keeping his discussion of it separate from the communism of women and children, Aristotle makes it an attack not just on Plato, but on the communism of property generally.

7. This is not to say Aristotle does defend a system of unqualified privatization, only that such a system would fall under option 1. As we shall see, there are many particular property arrangements that fall under each of these three broad arrangements.

8. On whom Aristotle might be referring to when he mentions some nations and some barbarians, see Newman (1887, 2:245-46).

9. Also, the examples are narrow, dealing with crops and land alone. Other kinds of arrangements might be broader, or narrow in a different way.

10. Barnes (1990, 252) writes that "Aristotle's remarks [on property] in the *Politica* are too nebulous to sustain any serious critical discussion." Some scholars are

(a bit) more confident about successfully getting to the bottom of Aristotle's opinions concerning property, but few have dealt with the topic in any detail. (Miller [1991] and [1995, ch. 9] are important exceptions.) I hope in this chapter to prove Barnes wrong.

11. Aristotle says "farmers" but he probably means "farmers, and any others who do hard work."

Newman (1887, 2:246) in a note on *heterón* quite correctly points out: "'others than the citizens,' not, I incline to think, 'others than the owners,' though the two meanings do not lie far apart." (Cf. Schütrumpf [1991, 2:17, 195].)

12. *Apolausis* means "act of enjoying," "fruition," "result of enjoying," "pleasure" (Liddell, Scott, and Jones, s.v.), and here most likely refers to the enjoyment of, or benefit from, some thing. (See Schütrumpf [1991, 2:195].)

13. Although Aristotle says the one who works hard deserves more rewards (and here he must mean material rewards), he does not make the Lockean connection between labor and the right to property—the right to that with which I have mixed my labor.

The connection between honor and material reward was central in Homer's *Iliad*. (See the passage quoted at the opening of this chapter, as well as IX 104-13. Cf. *NE* 1163b5-14.)

14. Newman (1887, 2:246) writes:

> If those who till the soil are not citizens but a separate and subordinate class . . . , disagreements would be less likely to result from the citizens holding property in common, for, as the citizens would not work themselves, individual citizens would not be in a position to compare their own hard work and small recompense with the easy work and large recompense of others, and thus one main source of disagreement among the citizens would be removed.

Newman is right. Slaves are under the control of others and thus have to do what they are told. Moreover, there is no justice or injustice, really, in one's relation to one's slaves. (See *Pol.* 1254a8-15, *NE* 1134b9-11.)

This arrangement is easier to manage, and Aristotle prefers it. Nevertheless, he does not believe that it is entirely unproblematic. At *Pol.* 1269a34-b12, he points out that slaves, serfs, and helots sometimes revolt and that generally the supervision of them is troublesome. The solution seems to be to find the middle path between being too lax with them, which leads to arrogance and a belief among them that they merit an equal standing, and being too harsh, which leads them to hate, and revolt against, their masters.

15. For examples of those who accept this interpretation, see Newman (1887, 2:246-47); Susemihl and Hicks (1894, 233); Bornemann (1923, 141-42); Barker (1958, 55-56); Aubonnet (1960, 138). See also Schütrumpf (1991, 2:195).

16. A more common objection to this criticism of Plato—levelled against Aristotle by, for example, all those mentioned in the previous note—is that Aristotle assumes there will be a communism of property among the iron and bronze class when, it is claimed, this is obviously not the case. But again, see the appendix.

17. Bornemann (1923) seems to hold such a view of Aristotle.

18. Although Aristotle does not mention jointly owned property, it may have been on his reader's mind, for disputes were known to arise over such arrangements. (See *AC* 52.2, 56.6, Rhodes [1993, 585-86, 631], Harrison [1968, 1:239-43].)

19. The key phrase—*mallon d' epidōsousin* (1263a28)—can be translated in two ways. First, *mallon* can be translated as "more": "but they will increase (give, contribute, advance, etc.) more." Some who translate it this way take the passage to mean that the land cultivated privately will produce more (and I think that is certainly close to Aristotle's meaning). See Newman (1887, 2:248) and Susemihl and Hicks (1894, 235). Barker (1958) believes that Aristotle means the amount of interest citizens have will increase.

I go with the second way of translating *mallon*, as "rather": "but rather they will improve (grow, advance, etc.)." I take this quite generally: they will simply do better under these circumstances. Why will they do better? Because they will be less prone to fight and more likely to produce more.

20. Aristotle seems to offer this as a major reason why property should be private. (Cf. Saunders [1995], 120: "[Aristotle does not] defend private property . . . on the grounds of economic efficiency or productivity. . . .") Note that this passage from Aristotle follows directly after his claim that property should be private generally, and is linked to it with a *gar*.

21. For *euprosōpos*, Liddell, Scott, and Jones gives as a general meaning "fair of face," and I have translated it accordingly. But Liddell, Scott, and Jones also lists "fair in outward show," "specious." Newman (1887, 2:253) says it means "wears a plausible look," and Saunders (1992, 115-16) might be right in thinking it here means "sounds attractive when first hearing about it."

22. This list is not necessarily exhaustive. Although Aristotle does not mention theft here, it makes sense to think he had it in mind. (See the following note.)

23. See *Rep.* 425c-e, 464d-465c, and Aristophanes, *Eccl.* 560-67, 605-7, 655-73. Both works mention the elimination of theft.

24. See *Pol.* 1263a15-21. On why the fact that those who share property in common quarrel more has not been persuasive evidence against communism, Aristotle writes: "But we observe few of those at odds from sharing in common when we compare them to the many who possess possessions privately" (*Pol.* 1263b25-27). To give a simple example: If there were 1,000 people who owned property privately, and we saw 10 percent of them at odds with each other over property, we would see 100 people having these difficulties. If there were 100 people who shared property in common, and we saw 50 percent of them at odds over their property, we would see 50 people having various difficulties. We would thus see more private property owners in trouble than those who held property in common. But this obviously does not count in favor of communism (as some seem to think) because if all (1,100) people were made to share property in common, we would expect there to be 550 having the difficulties Aristotle mentions—far higher than what we would expect if property were private (namely, 110).

25. Communism is a form of property leveling, and some claim that it cures crime. Thus Aristotle's discussion in *Pol.* II 7 seems applicable.

26. Not all factional conflict is due to unequal property. (See *Pol.* 1266b38-1267a2.)

27. On painless pleasures, see *NE* 1152b36-1153a2, 1173b15-19, 1177a25-26, *PA* 645a7-19. It is unclear whether Aristotle has in mind the committing of crimes in order to study (which seems rather strange), or some other kind of crime (e.g., tyranny). He may be thinking of the view that a tyrant could experience any pleasure with ease or without pain. See Xenophon, *Hiero*.

28. Number (1) is ensured by common meals and every citizen owning land and other property. Number (2) is ensured by laws and moral education. (More on these later.)

29. This passage continues: "Being a lover of self (*philauton*) is justly blamed. But this is not to have affection for oneself (*to philein heauton*), but having more affection than one ought, just as in the case of the money lover, since almost everyone has affection for each of these things" (1263b2-5). Here, Aristotle distinguishes a lover of self from a person who loves (or has affection for) himself. In the *Rhetoric*, however, he treats the two interchangeably (as we shall see).

30. *Eleutheros* can mean "speaking or acting like a freeman," "liberal," "generous" (i.e., "giving freely"), or "free." (*Eleutheria* can mean "freedom," "liberty," "license," "generosity.") Obviously, we are concerned with the term as it refers to the giving of property freely.

31. At this point, Aristotle actually mentions the destruction of two virtues: generosity and moderation (*Pol.* 1263b8-11). But we shall be interested in the former alone. Aristotle's discussion of moderation (*sôphrosunê*) is better suited to his treatment of the communism of women and children than it is to the communism of property because the moderation he claims is destroyed under communism is "moderation concerning women." He adds: "it is a fine deed to abstain from another's woman through moderation" (*Pol.* 1263b9-11). The argument he is making would therefore look something like this: (1) Under the communism of women, there is no such thing as "another's woman" (or "my woman"). (2) Therefore, under the communism of women, one never abstains from another's woman through moderation. (3) It is a fine thing to abstain from another's woman through moderation (rather than not abstaining at all, or abstaining through compulsion). (4) Therefore, the communism of women destroys a fine thing. Although valid, this argument is quite limited. It applies to adultery alone, not to sex generally (i.e., heterosexual and homosexual activity, sex with wives, prostitutes, etc.), nor does it apply to food and drink, or money and possessions. (According to both Aristotle and Plato, moderation applies to all these things. See *NE* 1117b25-1118b1, *EE* 1230b21-1231a25, *Pol.* 1265a28-38, *Rep.* 389d-390a, 402e-403a, 416d, 485e, 555c, 559b-c, 571d, 591d-e.) So if Aristotle were concerned here solely with attacking the communism of women, then we would have to admit that this criticism is not very powerful: The guardians will not have the opportunity to exercise their moderation in relation to some women. (At a certain point, the guardians can have sex with whomever they please among the guardians. See *Rep.* 461b-c.) Aristotle says that moderation is needed in the city, both for occupations and leisure, especially when a city has all the necessary goods for living well (*Pol.* 1334a11-b5). He also claims that moderation is a remedy for crime (*Pol.* 1267a10). These may be the works of moderation he thinks are destroyed by communism.

32. Stalley (1991, 195-96) writes:

Bornemann [1923, 143-44] (following Schlosser [*Aristoteles Politik* (Leipzig, 1798), 109]) claims that one can show liberality [i.e., generosity] as much in voluntarily renouncing property as in its use. Even if we leave on one side the question whether a Platonic guardian could be said voluntarily to have renounced property, this still misses the point. For Aristotle active friendship is part of human well-being. We therefore need private property, in order that we may bestow benefits on our friends.

33. This is in part the point of Aristotle's criticism of the communism of women and children in *Pol.* II 3-4, discussed in chapter 4.

34. Aristotle is using "generosity" (*eleutheria*) narrowly here to refer to the giving of possessions (see *Pol.* 1263b11). In *NE* IV 1, generosity is described as the virtue concerning the giving (and taking) of wealth, where wealth is anything whose value or worth is measured in money (1119b22-27). This could arguably include generosity with one's time and labor, for instance. Such generosity (broadly understood) will not fall to Aristotle's criticism, although the narrow sense will. Of course, Plato could argue (in fact, he probably would argue) that the narrow sense of generosity is not a virtue in his best city, and thus the argument that generosity will not exist there proves nothing of importance.

35. One must keep in mind that Aristotle's opinion of Sparta is in general quite negative. See especially *Pol.* II 9.

36. Aristotle or an anonymous student of Aristotle. Rhodes (1993) supports the latter, Keaney (1992) the former.

37. Compare this passage from *AC* 27.3 to 16.2-4 (and see Rhodes [1993, 214-15]).

Aristotle is very likely contrasting this private generosity with the public generosity (i.e., the "generosity" with public funds; see *AC* 27.4) of Pericles. (See Rhodes [1993, 339]; cf. *NE* 1120a34-b1.) (Aristotle would not have found Cimon's providing the poor with sustenance ideal, preferring instead a system of common meals. More will be said on this later.)

The generosity of Cimon might bring to mind public service or liturgies (*leitourgia*). But did Aristotle approve of them and/or include them in his conception of common use? Carter (1986, 41) writes that in Athens during the classical period, "the performance of civic duties had grown from something more casual, even amateur, to something highly professional and full-time." This may very well have been true of liturgies too, for they had become obligatory (though many were done voluntarily). Although Aristotle may not have minded voluntary liturgies, he did object to compulsory ones (see *NE* IV 2, *Pol.* 1309a14, f89R3 = Cicero, *de Officiis* II 16.56-57).

For some interesting remarks on the ways in which a person can and cannot help himself to the fruit of another, see Plato, *Laws* 844d-845d.

38. In the example from Lakedaimon at *Pol.* 1263a35-37, Aristotle mentions provisions *for travel* from the farms. This may suggest that putting one's land to common use was something he regarded as ad hoc rather than something relied upon for the general maintenance of the needy.

39. Tarentum was a colony of Sparta and thus very likely had many of the institutions Aristotle gives as examples at *Pol.* 1263a35-37. See Newman (1887, 4:536-37).

40. These are not mutually exclusive categories. There could be laws against theft—laws compelling me not to steal—and yet I choose not to steal voluntarily. What I am asking here is this: Is my giving of property to others simply voluntary, or must I

give certain things to others according to the law (and is this what Aristotle means by common use)?

41. See *Pol.* 1263a22-40, 1329b41-1330a2. Virtuous actions are voluntary, not forced (*NE* 1109b30-1110a1).

42. I see no reason for accepting Nussbaum's translation "common by way of a use that is agreed upon in mutuality" (1990, 203). Liddell, Scott, and Jones gives "friendly" for *philikos* and says *philikôs* is the opposite of *polemikôs*.

43. This promise is not fulfilled in the *Politics* that has come down to us.

44. Aristotle is asking: If we could set up a city in the best way possible, how should we do it? All he is talking about is the original distribution of land in the city. (He may have in mind the rather common phenomenon of colonization. Cf. Plato, *Laws* 737b-c; see Wycherley [1976, 4-5, 210-11n3].) We must be very cautious about trying to derive strong principles of redistribution from what Aristotle says here, as does Nussbaum, for example. See Nussbaum (1988, 147-84, with a reply to Charles, 207-14), e.g., p. 172, and (1990), e.g., p. 210. But this having been said, I think Charles (1988, 203-4) goes a bit too far when he states that "we have no idea as to what specific policies of distribution Aristotle would favour. That is, for all he says, he might have preferred either a minimal or maximal state, Rawlsian or Nozickian or Marxist principles of distribution." I believe that in the end, as unclear as Aristotle's own position is, we can rule out its being either "Nozickian" or Marxist. That is, Aristotle defends neither the absolutism of property rights, which entails no (or almost no) limitations on the ownership of property, nor the extremely limited ownership of property, which includes a great deal of redistribution.

45. Cf. *Pol.* 1265b24-27; see Plato, *Laws* 745e. I shall not be concerned with the city-frontier distinction.

It is this private land, of course, along with the citizens' private possessions, that will (hopefully) be used in common in the way Aristotle describes. How the public lands are used, however, falls outside of Aristotle's conception of "private property, common use."

46. The relevant Greek lines, describing the two divisions of the territory, are (*Pol.* 1330a9-11): (1) *anagkaion eis duo merê diêirêsthai tên chôran*, and (2) *kai toutôn hekateran diêirêsthai dicha palin*. Nussbaum translates them: (1) "we must divide the land into two portions," and (2) "we must divide each of these two portions in half (*dicha*) again." I would translate them: (1) "it is necessary to divide the territory into two parts," and (2) "[it is necessary] to divide each of these [two parts] in two (*dicha*) again." There is no mention of equal parts. *Dicha* does not necessarily mean "two equal parts" (see Liddell, Scott, and Jones, *Top.* 142b12-19, *HA* 503a28, *PA* 644a11), though it sometimes can (see *Pol.* 1318a40). For *NE* 1132a28, Bonitz (1870) writes: "*in duas partes pares*," but that is by no means necessary. (Cf. *Phys.* 239b19.) So we have no way of telling what Aristotle intended (or even whether his intentions were ever so specific). We know the territory in a city that aims at being best must be divided into four parts, but we cannot know (at least not from this passage) the relative size of these parts. (Actually, it is very unlikely the parts are equal. Will one fourth of all the land be set aside for service to the gods?)

47. On funds from mines, see *AC* 22.7, Rhodes (1993, 277-9), Harrison (1968, 1:234).

48. Newman (1887, 2:354) writes: "The term *phoroi* applied to the contributions of the serfs indicates subjection, and probably conquest." We need not assume that Aristotle is advocating or counting on the collection of tribute from such subjects, although we cannot rule it out.

Athens had as many as 350 or so tribute paying allies (not necessarily subjects), including most member states of the Delian League. (See *AC* 24.3, Rhodes [1993, 300-302].) This may have been another legitimate means of income for the city, in Aristotle's view, but once again we cannot say for sure.

49. Clearly, Aristotle wants the common funds to ensure the participation of poor citizens in the common meals. (See Nussbaum [1990, 204, 228], Irwin [1987, 46].) Here, Aristotle's ideal parts company from common practice. Ephoros (quoted in Strabo X 4.16) states that in Crete the common funds paid for boys and the poor. Pyrgion, also discussing Crete, says orphans are taken care of by the common funds (Athenaeus 143e). It is never claimed that the common funds support all citizens, unless the contributions of those who can afford it are considered part of the common funds. According to Dosiadas, every citizen contributes one tenth of his income to help support the common meals (Athenaeus 143a-d). Aristotle, however, is hoping the common lands will produce enough so that no one will have to contribute anything for the maintenance of the common meals.

50. See Athenaeus 143a, Plutarch, *Lycurgus* XII 7, Xenophon, *LC* V 7.

51. For the presence of boys at common meals, see Strabo X 4.20, Athenaeus 143a-e, Plutarch, *Lycurgus* XII 4, Xenophon, *LC* V 5-6. (On some possible doubts about common meals for the young, see Plato, *Laws* 636b-e, 666b.) On women, see Athenaeus 143a-d, Plato, *Rep.* 458c-d. Although there are common meals for women in neither Sparta nor Crete, it seems Plato and Aristotle think there should be separate ones for them. See Plato, *Laws* 780d-781d, 806d-807b, Aristotle, *Pol.* 1265a8-9.

52. One last point: Is attendance at the common meals voluntary or compulsory? In Sparta, they were, with minor exceptions, compulsory. (See Plutarch, *Lycurgus* XII 2-3; cf. Plato, *Laws* 762b-c.) But Aristotle's view is unclear, for his position is never fully stated. If their sole purpose is to ensure that the poor have enough to eat, then all that is necessary is that they be available, not mandatory. If they have some other purpose(s), then he may have thought they should be compulsory. It is unlikely that the sole purpose of the common meals was the maintenance of the poor. There was probably something about participation in the common meals (besides getting a decent meal) that Aristotle found important for all citizens. One possibility is education: The common meals may have had some role in the formation of the character of citizens, for instance, letting the young observe the proper way of conducting oneself in a social context. (As we have seen, Aristotle never fulfilled his promise to say more about common meals. *Pol.* VIII, which is about education, is generally considered incomplete. Perhaps the rest of Aristotle's discussion of common meals was [or was intended to be] in this book on education. If this is the case, then common meals obviously have an educational function.) If this was the case, then they may have been compulsory. A related purpose is the nurturing of civic friendship. The unity of the city depends on civic friendship, which in turn requires that citizens spend time together and gain knowledge of each other. Common messes would provide an excellent opportunity for this. (See, for instance, *Pol.* 1313a41-b6, *NE* 1155a23-26, 1167a22-28. The *Laws* mentions education in courage and

moderation [625c-626a, 635e-636a].) In the end, however, it is quite unclear whether common meals in Aristotle's view were meant to be compulsory, though most likely he would have hoped that people in the best city would be of such a character that they would voluntarily participate in them.

53. Compare this to Theophrastus' *Nomoi*, which states that "the market-inspectors (*agoranomous*) must look after two things: (a) good order in the market place, and (b) honest dealing not only by the sellers but also by the buyers" (f. 20). (Fragment numbers refer to the arrangement of fragments in Szegedy-Maszak [1987], from which this translation is taken.) For an earlier, and not dissimilar, view of market-inspectors, see Plato, *Laws* 759a, 764b, 849a-e, 881b-c, 913d, 917b-e, 920c, 936c, 953b.

54. See *Pol.* 1321b34-40, Theophrastus, *Nomoi* f. 21. For what is probably a very accurate description of their functions, see Newman (1887, 4:549).

For *eukosmia*, Liddell, Scott, and Jones gives "orderly behaviour," "good conduct," and "decency."

55. On the functions of this office, cf. Plato, *Laws* 759a, 763c, 779c, 844b-c, 845e, 847a-b, 849a-b, e, 879d-e, 881c, 913d-914c, 936c, 954b-c.

56. *Pol.* 1266b8-16, 1270a15-22, 1295b1-1296a18, 1309a14-26, 1319a8-10, *AC* 11.2-12.3. He also believes some restrictions on the alienation of property are justified (*Pol.* 1270a18-21).

57. In Plato's *Laws*, any surplus above the limit goes to "the city and the gods who possess the city" (744e-745a).

58. See *Pol.* 1258b35-39, 1328b39-41, 1337b8-15. Aristotle may have, in some circumstances, condoned the ostracism of the wealthy. See *Pol.* 1284a17-22, 1284b15-34, 1308b19; but cf. 1302b15-20. On the Peripatetic view of ostracism, see Szegedy-Maszak (1987, 52-54) and Miller (1995, 245-47).

59. *Pol.* 1283a16-19, 1328b10-23; cf. *AC* 24.3.

60. And, to some degree, the habits of (some?) adults. For example, laws making them act moderately. (See *NE* 1180a1-18.)

61. That education is the responsibility of the legislator, see *Pol.* VIII 1, *NE* 1102a7-10, 1130b25-29, X 9.

62. But cf. *NE* 1180a32-b31.

63. This passage seems to conflict with what I have claimed are Aristotle's views on individual independence. I believe there are three ways of interpreting the passage in light of this apparent contradiction: First, Aristotle is contradicting himself. In some places he says a free man is of himself and not of another (see *Pol.* 1254a10-15, *Met.* 982b25-26), whereas here he is saying a free man is not of himself but of another (of the city), which counts as despotic rule. (See Irwin [1987, 44n2] and [1988, 419-20].) Second, however contradictory Aristotle may appear, this passage is strong evidence for the view that he really saw humans as mere parts of the city. (This is the position of Barnes [1990, 262-63], who uses this passage as part of an argument for the view that Aristotle is an implicit totalitarian.) Third, Aristotle is here presenting the relationship between the individual and the city *in one special context*: the education of the young. Generally a citizen does belong to himself, but because he is a part of the city (in the looser sense) and has an interest in the end or aim of the city, and because the common education of the city is crucial to achieving that end, in this context alone he should not *consider*

(*nomizein*) himself as his own, but as the city's. Although I cannot argue for it here, this is the view I accept.

64. Education contributes to the unity of the city in the following ways: (1) Making education the same for all tends to give all citizens the same type of character—the one appropriate for the given constitution (*Pol.* VIII 1). This helps to preserve the city—to keep it whole (*Pol.* 1310a12-14, 1337a14-16). (2) Education tends to endow citizens with virtues that enable them to live a shared life together, e.g., justice and generosity (*NE* 1095b4-6, 1102a7-10, 1130b25-29, 1180a5-18).

Conclusion

"Society" is such a dangerous abstraction. As a rule, what can pass for a benefit to "society" is actually a disaster to all and any single individuals composing it. As witness Soviet Russia. I cannot get away from the idea that "society" as such does not exist, apart from its members. It is not a separate, mystical entity. It is only a shorter way of saying "a million" or "hundred million people." Yet all collectivist schemes use the word State or Society as a complete, single entity and demand that all individual citizens sacrifice everything for it. If we have a society where everyone sacrifices—just exactly who profits and who is happy? A happy collective composed of miserable, frustrated members is an absurdity. . . . You cannot claim that you have a healthy forest composed of rotting trees. I'm afraid that the collectivists cannot see the trees for the forest.

Ayn Rand, Letter to John Temple Graves, August 12, 1936 (ten years after she left Russia)

Politics II 5 (1264b15-24): Wholes, Parts, and Happiness

The third book of the *Republic* ends with Socrates' description of the communal and ascetic lifestyle of the rulers. At the beginning of book IV, Adeimantus chastises Socrates for not making the rulers—who are the best people in the city—happy. Socrates responds:

It would not be surprising if these men, living in such a way, are happiest (*eudaimonestatoi*) as well. In founding the city, though, we are not looking to which group among us will be especially happy, but as far as possible to the whole city. . . . We are forming a happy city, not taking a [happy] few and putting them in it (420b).

Aristotle's last criticism of the communism of the *Republic* is leveled against Socrates' response to Adeimantus:

> He even destroys the happiness of the guardians, saying the lawgiver should make the whole city happy. But it is impossible for a whole to be happy unless most or all or some of the parts have happiness. For being happy is not of the same [class of things] as evenness. It is possible for this to belong to the whole but to neither of the parts, but it is impossible for happiness. But if the guardians are not happy, then which others are? For the craftsmen and the multitude of the vulgar certainly are not (1264b15-24).

Happiness is not the same kind of characteristic as evenness: it cannot belong to the whole without also belonging to the parts. For example, the number eight is even, but it can be broken up into two parts (five and three); five and three are odd numbers. But this is not the case with the happiness of a city. A city can be happy or flourishing only if its parts (or most or some [but not just a few] of its parts) are also happy or flourishing. We judge the happiness of a city by reference to how well the individuals within it are doing. A city is, after all, a collection of *individuals*, and it exists for the sake of *their* happiness.

Scholars have generally viewed Aristotle's remarks as quite unfair to Plato, who does, after all, go to great lengths—especially in *Rep.* IX—to show that the rulers most of all will be happy. (See also 465e-466c.)[1] But this misses the point. Aristotle is criticizing Plato's basic approach to political philosophy, an approach that runs throughout the *Republic*: that of treating the citizens of a city as mere parts—like the parts of a substance or the parts of a household, not as independent individuals—and the city itself as a whole with an end or ends above or beyond the ends of the individuals within the city. It does not really matter, Aristotle could reply, that Plato later states that the rulers (and all the other citizens) will be happy. Aristotle believes that for all the reasons we have seen, Plato's approach is absolutely wrongheaded. A happy city depends on happy *individuals*. It is this focus on individuals that, in Aristotle's view, Plato has overlooked. This is no doubt why Aristotle presented this particular criticism last: It is a fitting conclusion to his critique of Plato's *Republic*.

Implications for Aristotle's Political Philosophy

At the beginning of this book I said it was my hope: (1) to discover what exactly (philosophically) Aristotle was saying in his (often obscure) criticisms of Plato's *Republic* in *Pol.* II 1-5; and (2) to show that these chapters are important (and thus deserve more attention than they have received) because they deal with what turns out to be an important issue: the unity of the city. I believe I have accomplished these aims.

But in connection with this second point, I also said that one reason these chapters are important is that they can help us in attempting to characterize Aristotle's political philosophy. In conclusion, I should like to reiterate briefly what light *Pol.* II 1-5 sheds on the nature of his political philosophy, primarily by pointing out two views of his *Politics* that I believe these chapters rule out.

Jonathan Barnes, in an article entitled "Aristotle and Political Liberty" (1990), stipulates that a person enjoys political liberty in those areas where the state does not intervene (250). Unfortunately, he claims, Aristotle does not deal directly with the issues of political liberty and limitations on the government (251, 258-59). But there is, Barnes says, nonetheless a tendency in Aristotle towards totalitarianism, for Aristotle holds that the state has a role to play (or at least the authority to play a role) in every (or almost every) area of human life (see especially 259-60).

It is beyond the scope of this brief conclusion to present and respond to all of Barnes's arguments;[2] however, I should like to respond briefly to one of his central claims. Barnes says that "Aristotle's implicit totalitarianism rests ultimately on . . . a metaphysical untruism" (263). The city may intrude into every aspect of my life because, according to Barnes's reading of Aristotle, I am essentially, by my very nature, a part of the city. This in the end is Aristotle's great error.

> In any event, are men of their States? Am I a part of, and am I of, the United Kingdom of Great Britain and Northern Ireland? In a loose enough sense of "part," maybe I am part of the Kingdom. But I am not a part in any ordinary sense: I do not stand to the Kingdom as my arm stands to my body or as a piece stands to a jigsaw puzzle or as a sparking-plug stands to a motor-car engine. For I am an independent individual. That, in the end, is the crucial fact about me (and about you), and it is a fact which, in the *Politica*, Aristotle ignores or suppresses (263).

A close study of *Pol.* II 1-5 shows that this claim is incorrect,[3] for such a study reveals a tendency *away* from totalitarianism, and a respect for individual independence. As we have seen, Aristotle believed in the importance of an individual's planning his own life, and he held that the proper unity of the city requires that adult citizens be treated as independent, separate, and separable components of a city, *not* as parts by nature, like the parts of an organism—nor even as parts of a household.

But given that Aristotle respects the need for individual independence among citizens, does this mean we should characterize him as a liberal or protoliberal?[4] Nussbaum (1980, 1988, 1990), it seems, would answer yes (for she sees a form of modern liberalism or social democracy in Aristotle's political philosophy). She believes Aristotle defends the need for individual autonomy (what I have been calling independence). But she also believes (and she believes Aristotle believes) such autonomy is inconsistent with freedom, if by freedom one means laissez-faire (1988, 212-13). Thus, in the case of education, for instance, the curtailment of some freedom actually leads to a greater freedom of choice. And this is one justification for Aristotle's theory of public education, which in her view includes an important role for parents and should not be considered coercive or paternalistic. In her view Aristotle's public education does not entail a decrease in autonomy (1988, 161, 168, 171, 212-13; 1990, 233-34).

In addition, Aristotle (in Nussbaum's view) advocates the distribution by the state of a wide range of goods to a broad group of people—not just the distribution of political offices to a small group of citizens (1988). (See the response from Charles [1988].) This distribution includes (or often requires) a possibly vast redistribution of wealth (1988, 172; 1990, 215). Indeed, in her view, Aristotle's position that adult citizens must possess a great deal of autonomy depends on private property *not* being held absolutely. Whatever property we do "own" is provisional, qualified, subject to the claims of need (1990, 204-5, 231-32).

Although we both see in Aristotle a fundamental concern for independence or autonomy, there are important differences between my view and Nussbaum's. First, I believe the education of the young discussed in *Pol.* VIII 1 can only accurately be described as coercive. Given the importance of character and, moreover, the importance of a common character throughout the citizenry, Aristotle believes (in the context of education alone) that adult citizens must regard themselves as mere parts of the city—not as independent individuals for whom it is best to plan their own lives and the lives of their families. Nussbaum is right. Parents will no doubt have an important role to play in the upbringing of their children (see *NE* X 9), but it will be a subordinate role. The father cannot rely strictly on his own choices and his own judgment. (See Charles [1988, 202-4].)

So the freedom and independence Aristotle advocates depends upon or requires a coercive system of public education (and, I should add, the leisure that only slave or barbarian labor can provide). I believe this is enough to rule out labeling Aristotle a liberal in any essential way.

I also think Nussbaum is incorrect with regard to property. As I have shown, Aristotle does not think that (in the best city, at least) a strictly controlled system of property is a condition for autonomy or independence; rather, he believes that a system of private property—where one truly possesses and controls his own property—is not only most efficient and just, it also better enables one to live an independent life. For instance, when others are benefited through their use of my property, it is not because I have been forced to give my property to others by law, but because I am of such character that I have, by my own choice and through the control of my own property, decided to share it with others.

In summary, how should we characterize Aristotle's political philosophy? It is difficult using modern terminology. Suffice it to say that he believes a rather high degree of individual independence is necessary for the fullest human life (and in this sense perhaps we can call his political philosophy "liberal"). But it is also true that this life is not possible to everyone and that it must be paid for by some rather "unliberal" institutions, for example, his system of public education. I believe this picture of Aristotle's political thought is accurate but that it cannot be arrived at completely nor fully understood without a careful study and proper understanding of *Pol.* II 1-5.

Notes

1. See Susemihl and Hicks (1894, 244), Adam (1902, 1:206), Saunders (1992, 113). Stalley (1991, 197-98) is mixed. Bornemann (1923, 150), commenting on this passage, asks: "Hat Aristoteles wirklich Platons Politeia gelesen, oder kennt er sie vielleicht nur vom Hörensagen?"

2. Earlier I criticized some of the points made in Barnes (1990). For a fuller critique of Barnes, see Sorabji (1990).

3. Barnes writes that in attempting to discover evidence to answer the charge that Aristotle is a totalitarian, the criticism of Plato's *Republic* in *Pol.* II 1-5 is a red—"or at least pinkish"—herring (251-52). I obviously disagree.

4. "Liberalism," as it is used today, is unfortunately a very vague term. It ranges in meaning from laissez-faire classical liberalism to modern welfare liberalism.

Appendix

Aristotle on the Extent of Platonic Communism

In *Pol.* II 5, Aristotle writes:

> what the scheme of the whole constitution will be for those sharing in it, Socrates has not said, nor is it easy to say. And yet the multitude of the city [i.e., all the citizens] turns out to be nearly [the same as] the multitude of the other citizens [i.e., the iron and bronze citizens], concerning whom nothing has been determined, whether among the farmers as well possessions should be common or private to each individual, and further, whether women and children should be private or common (1264a11-17).

Aristotle thus believes that it is unclear in the *Republic* how the members of the lower class (who constitute the vast majority of citizens) are to live.[1]

Most modern scholars, however, hold that it is quite clear that the lower class is not to live communistically. Barker (1958, 52n4), for instance, writes that "Aristotle here [1264a11-17] forgets, or at any rate neglects, the actual argument of the *Republic*. Plato makes it clear that the farmers own private property, and live in private or separate families." And Aubonnet (1960, 142n6) says "Platon . . . indique clairement que la communauté des biens ne s'applique pas à l'ensemble des citoyens et il apparait clairement que la communauté des femmes, des enfants et des biens ne concerne que les gardes." This same position is held in one form or another, explicitly or implicitly, by Grote (1865, 3:207-8), Newman (1887, 1:159), Susemihl and Hicks (1894, 215), Bornemann (1923, 113-18), Shorey (1930, 1:xxxiv, 462), Popper (1971, 48), Mulgan (1977, 29), Strauss (1978, 113-15), Annas (1981, 178), Reeve (1988, 184), Price (1989, 179), Stalley (1991, 186), Saunders (1992, 103), and Waterfield (1994, xxxiii). The reasons generally given for this view (when reasons are given) seem to be the following: (1) Socrates frequently speaks of his proposals as applying to the rulers without any suggestion that they would apply to anyone else (in fact, the entire discussion of communism comes up only when Socrates is discussing the rulers); and (2) some of the arguments he uses could apply only to the rulers. These two points certainly count as evidence, but are they enough to support their conclusion?

I do not think so. I believe Aristotle is right, and his modern critics wrong. A consideration of some key passages from the *Republic* shows that the question of how the lower class is to live (and particularly, whether the lower class is to live communistically) has not been fully or clearly answered by Plato's Socrates and that Aristotle is therefore justified in thinking it unresolved.

Since most scholars think it is clear that the communism of the *Republic* applies to the rulers alone and that the lower class lives in a manner that should not be described as communistic, I shall defend Aristotle's position by showing that (1) Socrates' proposals are consistent with there being some form of communism for the lower class; and (2) the idea of a communistic lower class is in fact more compatible with certain passages than the alternative view. But I shall not be more specific than this, i.e., I am not going to prove that a certain view of the *Republic* is correct. Aristotle's point is simply that Plato's position is not clear, and that is all I shall try to defend.

I shall treat the communism of women and children and the communism of property separately (see *Pol.* 1262b40-41), starting with the communism of women and children.

From the discussion of the rulers in book V of the *Republic*, we see that it is indisputable that a communism of women and children will exist among the rulers (457c-466c). "All these women [i.e., the female guardians] are to be common (*koinas*) to all these men [i.e., the male guardians], and no woman is to live privately with any man. And the offspring too will be common, and neither is a parent to know his own offspring, nor a child his parent" (457c-d). This communism is radical. The rulers will live in common houses, without private spouses, children, or relatives. (See 458c-d, 464b-e, 465b-c, 466c.)

As we shall see later, the lower class does not live according to this radical communism of women and children. There are, however, passages (outside of book V) referring to the communism of women and children that do not explicitly apply to the rulers alone and are in fact consistent with a communism of women and children among the lower class. Consider the first mention of the communism of women and children, in book V: "For if, being well educated, they become moderate [or reasonable, *metrioi*] men, they will easily see to all these things [e.g., limitations on wealth and property] and the other things that we are now leaving aside: that the possession of women, marriage, and the procreation of children must all to the highest degree be arranged according to the proverb that friends have all things in common" (423e-424a). And at the beginning of book VIII there is a brief summary of the city described in books IV-

V: "This has been agreed to, Glaucon: for the city that is going to be governed on a high level, women will be common, children and their entire education will be common, and similarly the practices in war and in peace will be common, and their kings will be those who are best in philosophy and with a view to war" (543a).[2] Neither of these passages singles out the gold and silver classes, nor do their respective contexts force us to conclude that the rulers alone are meant. True, the common practices in war no doubt apply to the rulers alone (see *Rep.* 466c-467a), but we cannot say the same about the second passage generally. In fact, since Plato says "their kings," one could argue that he most likely has the whole community in mind: the kings are the gold and silver men, for they are the best in philosophy and war; but it would be awkward to speak of "their kings" if all he had in mind were the kings themselves. This, however, though plausible, is by no means certain, for it could also be argued that Plato is contrasting the philosopher-rulers with the auxiliaries, or contrasting the rulers with the gold and silver youths who are not yet old enough to be kings.

Now one might argue that we should infer from the fact that the radical communism of women and children does not apply to the lower class that these more general passages must be speaking solely of the rulers as well. But this inference would be valid only if there was just the one type of communism of women and children—the radical one. But as Adeimantus says, there could be many kinds of communism of women and children (*Rep.* 449c-d). So the lower class might in some way share women and children in common, without it being the radical manner of the rulers.

As it turns out, some form of communism of women and children in the lower class is actually quite plausible when we consider the Myth of the Metals and the regulation of marriage, procreation, and children. Now clearly, the main discussion of the regulation of marriage, procreation, and children in book V refers only to the rulers, and this should not be surprising, as it is found in the context of a discussion of the radical communism of women and children (458d-461e). But let us consider the Myth of the Metals:

> "All of you in the city (*pantes hoi en têi polei*) are brothers" we shall say to them, presenting the myth, "but the god, forming those of you fit to rule, mixed gold in at their birth, for which they are most honored; and in the auxiliaries, silver; and iron and bronze in the farmers and the other craftsmen. Inasmuch as you are all related, while you will for the most part produce offspring like yourselves, it is sometimes the case that silver offspring will be born from a golden parent, and golden offspring from a silver parent, and likewise all the others from each other. Thus the god commands the rulers first and foremost that they will be good guardians of nothing and they will carefully guard nothing as [they will] the offspring, [seeing] which of these [metals] is mixed in their souls; and if a child of theirs should be born

bronze or iron underneath they are in no way to feel pity, but giving him the
honor fitting for his nature, they will thrust him out to the craftsmen or
farmers; and in turn, if from these any should grow [who are] golden or silver underneath, honoring them they will lead them up, some to the guardian
[class], others to the auxiliary [class], since there is an oracle that the city
will be destroyed when an iron man is its guardian or a bronze man guards
it" (*Rep.* 415a-c).

A bit later he writes: "If among the guardians some inferior child were born, he
would be sent away to the others, and if out of the others an excellent [child
were born], [he would be sent away] to the guardians" (423c-d).[3] Much is unclear about how the gold and silver children born among the lower class are to
be discovered. (The iron and bronze children born among the rulers will be
discovered in the course of the guardian education.) What is clear is that they
must be discovered early.[4] So, according to the Myth of the Metals, the guardians must have the power to observe all children, to take gold and silver children from the lower class and put them into a common nursery (or pen, *Rep.*
460c) for the gold and silver classes, and take iron and bronze children from
the rulers and thrust them upon the iron and bronze class (or upon some iron
and bronze family). This is best accomplished through some form of communism of women and children in the lower class. (In fact, it is hard to imagine a
noncommunist alternative.) Let us speculate along these lines.

There is a passage in Herodotus (of which Aristotle was most likely aware)
where a communism of women and children, of sorts, is described: "They [the
Auseans, a Libyan tribe] have sexual intercourse with their women in common
(*epikoinon*), and they do not live together [as couples], but have intercourse like
beasts. And when a woman's child is bigger [or full grown, *hadron*], within
three months the men come together in the same place, and the one of the men
the child resembles, everyone considers the child his" (IV 180; cf. *Pol.*
1262a19-21). Putting many details aside, some version of such a temporary
communism of women and children is certainly plausible, given what the Myth
of the Metals demands. That is, the monitoring of children from the lower class
is probably most easily managed if the children are raised in common, and only
after their "metal" is determined are they distributed to a more conventional
household. And since it is problematic to take children away from their biological parents, it would be easier simply to prevent strong natural family ties from
arising by immediately making the children common to all. This in turn might
be easier if men were not monogamous but had sexual intercourse with women
in common, and the women nursed and helped raise the children communally.
And then, after some time, each woman too would be assigned to a particular,
more traditional, household.

It is important to keep in mind the claim made at *Rep.* 460a that "the number of marriages will be left to the rulers, so that the number of men will remain approximately the same, taking into account wars, diseases, and all such things, and so that our city, as far as possible, will become neither too big nor too small." It seems clear that the regulation of "marriages" must exist for all classes. (Shorey [1930, 1:462] rather tendentiously comments: "Plato forgets that this legislation applies only to the guardians.")

The case for a communism of women is perhaps not terribly strong, but the idea is still quite plausible. However, the case for some kind of communism of children among the lower class is very strong indeed. Given that the *Republic* never says there is not a communism of women and children among the lower class, on this point at least Aristotle's remarks seem justified.

Now to the communism of property. Again, the rulers' lives are characterized by a radical communism.

> First, no one is to possess any private property, unless it is entirely necessary. Next, no one is to have any such house or storeroom into which everyone who wants cannot go. And the necessities, as much as moderate and courageous men training for war need, having been fixed as a payment from the other citizens, they are to receive as a wage for guarding, such an amount that in a year there is neither a surplus nor lack. And going to common meals like soldiers in a camp, they are to live a common life (*koinê zên*) (*Rep.* 416d-e; see 415e, 419a-420a, 458c-d, 464b-e, *Tim.* 18b).[5]

The lower class, however, is arranged quite differently. It is the money-making class: Members of the lower class produce goods or perform services, earn money, and exchange goods in the marketplace (*Rep.* 370e-371e, 415e, 434a-c, 441a, 463a-b, 547b-c). Can we conclude that there is definitely not a communism of property in the lower class? The passage following the one just cited certainly suggests an affirmative response: "But for [the guardians] of those in the city it is not lawful to handle or touch gold and silver, nor to go under the same roof [with it] nor to hang it around [themselves] nor to drink from gold or silver. And in this way they would be saved and they would save the city. *But if ever they possess private land, households, and currency, they will be householders and farmers instead of guardians*" (*Rep.* 417a). This passage is indeed very suggestive, but if one considers all that Plato has written (and especially *Rep.* 462a-e, which I shall look at shortly), it does not *rule out* the possibility of some kind of communism of property among the lower class (as Adam seems to think [1902, 1:200]). For this passage implies only that there is a clear difference between the rulers and the money-making class. The radical communism of the guardians rules out private land, households, and currency, but these are (as long as they are very limited, conditional, restricted) compatible with some other, more moderate, form of communism. Take, for instance, a city in which (most) land is common, but where there is some provisional private property.

The members of the lower class are clearly not left to their own devices: They cannot acquire money or wealth freely—they cannot become rich (*Rep.* 420d-421a).[6] Like the rulers, they are allowed only what their tasks require, but given the division of labor and the need for trade, their tasks require money. If ever they acquire money for its own sake, rather than as a means to an end, they would be money makers rather than farmers, craftsmen, shepherds, etc. (*Rep.* 341c, 342d, 345d, 397e, 551e-552a).[7] Therefore, the guardians must guard against wealth and poverty in the lower class: Poverty, because without money, craftsmen and farmers cannot purchase or maintain the tools of their trade, and because it tends to lead to innovation, wrongdoing, and a lack of generosity; wealth, because it leads to idleness, carelessness, luxury, and innovation (*Rep.* 421d-422a; cf. 552a-e).

The close control over the property and economic affairs of the lower class by the rulers is perhaps most efficiently handled through a communism of property of some kind (though we have seen that it cannot be the radical communism of property of the rulers). In his discussion of the different possible property arrangements, Aristotle mentions one in which property is owned in common but used in private. He gives an example: "The land is common and farmed in common, while the crops are divided with a view to private use" (*Pol.* 1263a5-7). Let us speculate, using this example as our model. Land is common or public, but it is divided for private use into many equal households for all members of the lower class. (They thus can be said in some sense to possess private households.) Further, farm land is common and farmed in common (or rather, divided into plots to be farmed individually). And the crops produced are divided among the farmers and the rest of the lower class (and even the guardian class—remember their "wage") for their private use, i.e., for sustenance, only as much as is needed. The farmers would also be given excess produce or money in order to acquire the rest of the things they need. With this unconsumed "private" property, the farmers are free to buy and sell goods in the marketplace, trading with others who have produced a surplus. Since the guardians are in charge of distribution they could ensure (as much as is possible) that members of the lower class do not acquire too much—more than is needed. (Cf. *Laws* 739e-740b.)

Certainly, other alternatives are possible and quite plausible. The management of the economic affairs of the lower class by the rulers might be handled just as well through laws regulating private property (for instance, by limiting the wealth and poverty of each citizen), rather than through a communism of property.[8] But again, given that the *Republic* never says there is not a communism of property of any kind among the members of the lower class, Aristotle's view that the *Republic* is unclear is justified.

At this point I want to consider a possible objection. Price (1989, 179) argues that "in the *Republic*, such communism is restricted to the guardians (who represent reason in the state) and the auxiliaries (who represent spirit . . .), perhaps for a reason suggested by E. Bornemann [1923, 123]: the imposition of communism on the artisans would undermine that motivation, appetite, which they represent, since property is an object of appetite (cf. 4.436a1-3, 8.553c5, 9.580e5-6)." All one need say in reply, however, is that the communism of the lower class must be arranged in such a way that it allows its members to satisfy their appetites (within limits, of course). But one could certainly imagine all the members of a communistic lower class having access to, for example, the things that characterize the feverish city of book II (couches, perfume, incense, cakes, ivory, etc.)—things that were added by Socrates (reluctantly) because not everyone would be satisfied by the goods of the healthy city (see *Rep.* 372a-373c).

In addition to the evidence I have surveyed, there is one last passage that I believe offers the strongest evidence for the view that Plato may have held that the lower class was arranged according to some form of communism. At *Rep.* 462a-e, Socrates says the greatest good for the city is what holds it together and makes it one, and the greatest evil what splits it apart. What holds the city together, he claims, is the community of pleasure and pain—when all say "mine" and "not mine" of the same things at the same time. What splits a city apart is privacy (including private spouses, children, and property). The city that possesses the most unity (along these lines) is the best. Whether Plato intended it or not, the logical implication of this passage is that full communism—a communism of women, children, and property among all citizens—is better than a communism that exists among the gold and silver classes only (see Stalley [1991, 186]). And in fact Plato does use expressions that suggest the whole city is intended: the communism of pleasure and pain involves "to the greatest extent all citizens" (*ho ti malista pantes hoi politai, Rep.* 462b); and, when one of us feels pain, "the entire community" (*pasa hê koinônia*) feels it as well (*Rep.* 462c; cf. 465b; see *Laws* 739c: *kata pasan tên polin hoti malista*).

What we have, in the end, is one very suggestive passage, as well as some circumstantial evidence, all of which support the view that Plato might have been committed to some kind of communism for the lower class as well as the gold and silver classes. I do not, however, think this evidence is conclusive (especially given *Rep.* 417a). On the contrary, I believe it is extremely difficult (if not impossible) to say with any certainty what precisely Plato had in mind for the lower class. And this after all is exactly what Aristotle asserts at *Pol.* 1264a11-17.

Notes

1. A possible problem: In *Pol.* II 4, Aristotle says that "the women and children being common would seem to be more useful to the farmers than to the guardians" (1262a40-b1). Newman (1887, 2:258) remarks that "Aristotle seems to take it for granted . . . that the community of women and children is to be confined to the guardians." Aubonnet (1960, 142n6) writes that "l'objection qu'Aristote élève en c. 4, 1260a40 [sic.] suiv. suppose que la communauté des femmes et des enfants se limite aux gardes" (cf. Adam [1902, 1:200]). But it is certainly possible that Aristotle is saying something like the following: "Plato, you have gone to a great deal of trouble to show us that the guardians should live communistically, whereas you have said very little about how the farmers should live, when in fact the farmers might benefit more from living communistically than the guardians." But this does not contradict Aristotle's claim in *Pol.* II 5 that it is unclear how the lower class in the *Republic* is to live.

2. See also *Laws* 739c-e, which is arguably a summary of the *Republic*. *Tim.* 17c-19a, which is certainly a summary of the *Republic*, clearly deals with the rulers alone, not the lower class, and thus is no help here.

3. Plato's account at places seems rather contradictory. First, at *Rep.* 460c he seems to advocate infanticide for iron and bronze children born among the gold and silver classes (but cf. *Tim.* 19a). Second, *Rep.* 463a-464a might be read to say that the guardians alone call each other brothers, sisters, fathers, etc. (which is not what we are led to believe at *Rep.* 415a; cf. 414e). But these contradictions do not count against Aristotle. If anything, they help to confirm his claim that Plato is unclear. (See the following note.)

4. Reeve (1988, 187) writes: "Clearly there would be no point in sending a child with iron or bronze in his psyche out among the farmers and craftsmen if he were there going to receive the very same education and honours as guardian offspring." In the same way, one might expect that the gold and silver children from the lower class must be sent to the rulers before the primary guardian education begins (unless everyone receives at least the first stages of this primary education). But in any case, at an early age some are marked for guardian education and some for technical training. (See, for instance, *Rep.* 467a and the secondary literature mentioned below.)

On the very controversial issue of whether all citizens receive the primary education of the guardians (or whether any born among the lower class do) see Reeve (1988, 186-91, 309n5), and Hourani (1949). There is no explicit statement in the *Republic*, and scholarly opinion varies widely. Hourani and Reeve reject the view that all citizens receive this education. Cornford (1941, 63-64), on the other hand, writes that "No explicit provision is made for their education; but unless they share in the early education provided for the Guardians, there could hardly be opportunities for promoting their most promising children to a higher order." Irwin (1977, 330-31n6) quite prudently holds that "Plato does not even make it clear who receives moral education. . . . Plato insinuates that the training will extend beyond the guardians, but he never says so." (Aristotle agrees with Irwin. See *Pol.* 1264a36-38.) The Myth of the Metals implies that gold and silver children will sometimes be born among the lower class and that these must be sent to the guardian class.

5. *Rep.* 419a–420a should *not* be taken as evidence that there is not a communism of property of any kind among the lower class. See Adam (1902, 1:205) and Reeve (1988, 185). Price (1989, 179n2) claims that "The restriction [of the communism to the gold and silver citizens] is most explicit in the recapitulation at *Timaeus* 18b1–4." (Cf. Newman [1887, 1:159n2].) But this passage says only that the rulers will possess no private property; it says nothing about the lower class.

6. *Rep.* 422d implies that there is to be *no* gold or silver in the city (at least none worth attacking the city for). Cf. *Rep.* 373a; see *Laws* 741e–742c.

7. But cf. *Rep.* 434a-b; see *Laws* 741e. Plato wants the members of the lower class to possess only as much as they need, though he most likely believes this limitation would be quite difficult to maintain or enforce, as they tend to be money lovers.

8. At *Rep.* 425c–427a, the interlocutors agree that they will not bother with laws concerning the marketplace, but will instead leave this sort of thing to the actual law-makers. This passage is compatible with both the communism of property and the strict regulation of private property.

Bibliography

Adam, J. 1902. *The Republic of Plato*. 2 vols. Cambridge: Cambridge University Press.

Adkins, A. W. H. 1960. *Merit and Responsibility: A Study in Greek Values*. Oxford: Oxford University Press.

Annas, J. 1981. *An Introduction to Plato's Republic*. Oxford: Oxford University Press.

——. 1990. "Comments on J. Cooper." In Patzig (1990), 242-48.

Aubonnet, J. 1960. *Aristote, Politique: Livres I et II*. Paris: Budé.

Barker, E. 1958. *The Politics of Aristotle*. 2nd ed. Oxford: Clarendon Press.

Barnes, J. 1990. "Aristotle and Political Liberty." In Patzig (1990), 249-63.

Barnes, J., ed. 1984. *The Complete Works of Aristotle: The Revised Oxford Translation*. 2 vols. Princeton: Princeton University Press.

Benardete, S. 1989. *Socrates' Second Sailing: On Plato's Republic*. Chicago: University of Chicago Press.

Bloom, A. 1968. *The Republic of Plato*. New York: Basic Books.

Bonitz, H. 1870. *Index Aristotelicus*. Berlin: de Gruyter.

Bornemann, E. 1923. "Aristoteles' Urteil über Platons politische Theorie." *Philologus* 79: 70-158, 234-57.

Burkert, W. 1985. *Greek Religion*. Trans. J. Raffan. Cambridge, Mass.: Harvard University Press

Cantarella, E. 1992. *Bisexuality in the Ancient World*. Trans. C. Ó Cuilleanáin. New Haven, Conn.: Yale University Press.

Carter, L. B. 1986. *The Quiet Athenian*. Oxford: Clarendon Press.

Cary, M. 1964. "Thebes." In J. Bury, S. A. Cook, and F. E. Adcock, eds. *The Cambridge Ancient History*. 2nd ed. Vol. 4. *Macedon, 401-301 B.C.*, 80-107. Cambridge: Cambridge University Press.

Charles, D. 1988. "Perfection in Aristotle's Political Theory: Reply to Martha Nussbaum." *Oxford Studies in Ancient Philosophy*. Supplementary Vol., 185-206. Oxford: Oxford University Press.

Cherniss, H. 1944. *Aristotle's Criticism of Plato and the Academy*. Baltimore: John Hopkins University Press.

————. 1964. *Aristotle's Criticism of Presocratic Philosophy*. 2nd ed. New York: Russell and Russell.

Connor, W. R. 1988. "'Sacred' and 'Secular': *Hiera kai hosia* and the Classical Athenian Concept of the State." *Ancient Society* 19: 171-85.

Cooper, J. M. 1980. "Aristotle on Friendship." In Rorty (1980), 301-40.

————. 1986. *Reason and Human Good*. 2nd ed. Indianapolis: Hackett.

————. 1990. "Political Animals and Civic Friendship." In Patzig (1990), 220-41.

Cornford, F. M. 1941. *The Republic of Plato*. Oxford: Oxford University Press.

Dobbs, D. 1985. "Aristotle's Anticommunism." *American Journal of Political Science* 29: 29-46.

Dover, K. J. 1974. *Greek Popular Morality in the Time of Plato and Aristotle*. Berkeley: University of California Press.

————. 1989. *Greek Homosexuality*. 2nd ed. Cambridge, Mass.: Harvard University Press.

Dreizehnter, A. 1970. *Aristoteles' Politica*. Munich: Wilhelm Fink.

Filmer, Robert. 1949. *Observations upon Aristotles Politiques Touching Forms of Government*. In P. Laslett, ed. *Patriarcha and the Other Political Writings of Sir Robert Filmer*. Oxford: Oxford University Press.

Gomme, A. W. 1956. *A Historical Commentary on Thucydides*. Vol. 2. Oxford: Oxford University Press.

Gotthelf, A. 1987. "First Principles in Aristotle's *Parts of Animals*." In A. Gotthelf and J. Lennox, eds. *Philosophical Issues in Aristotle's Biology*. Cambridge: Cambridge University Press.

Grote, G. 1865. *Plato, and the Other Companions of Socrates*. 3 vols. London: J. Murray.

Guthrie, W. K. C. 1981. *A History of Ancient Greek Philosophy*. Vol. 6. *Aristotle: An Encounter*. Cambridge: Cambridge University Press.

Halperin, D. M. 1990. *One Hundred Years of Homosexuality, and Other Essays on Greek Love*. New York: Routledge.

Hammond, N. G. L. 1986. *A History of Greece to 322 B.C.* Oxford: Oxford University Press.

Hammond, N. G. L. and H. H. Scullard, eds. 1970. *The Oxford Classical Dictionary*. 2nd ed. Oxford: Oxford University Press.

Harrison, A. R. W. 1968, 1971. *The Law of Athens*. 2 vols. Oxford: Oxford University Press.

Hourani, G. F. 1949. "The Education of the Third Class in Plato's *Republic*." *Classical Quarterly* 43: 58-60.

Irwin, T. 1977. *Plato's Moral Theory: The Early and Middle Dialogues*. Oxford: Oxford University Press.

————. 1985. *Aristotle: Nicomachean Ethics*. Indianapolis: Hackett.

————. 1987. "Generosity and Property in Aristotle's *Politics*." In E. Frankel Paul, F. Miller Jr., J. Paul, and J. Ahrens, eds. *Beneficence, Philanthropy and the Public Good*, 37-54. Oxford: Basil Blackwell.

————. 1988. *Aristotle's First Principles*. Oxford: Clarendon Press.

————. 1990. "Aristotle on the Good of Political Activity." In Patzig (1990), 73-98.

Keaney, J. J. 1981. "Aristotle, *Politics* 2.12.1274a22-b28." *American Journal of Ancient Greek History* 6: 97-100.

————. 1992. *The Composition of Aristotle's Athenaion Politeia: Observation and Explanation*. Oxford: Oxford University Press.

Keyt, D. 1987. "Three Fundamental Theorems in Aristotle's *Politics*." *Phronesis* 32: 54-79.

Liddell, H. G., and R. Scott. 1968. *Greek-English Lexicon*. Revised by H. S. Jones and R. McKenzie, with supplement. Oxford: Oxford University Press.

Lord, C. 1984. *Aristotle: The Politics*. Chicago: University of Chicago Press.

MacDowell, D. M. 1986. *The Law in Classical Athens*. Ithaca, N.Y.: Cornell University Press.

McInnes, N. 1972. "Communism." In P. Edwards, ed. *Encyclopedia of Philosophy*. New York: Macmillan.

Miller, F. D. 1983. "Rationality and Freedom in Aristotle and Hayek." *Reason Papers* 9: 29-36.

————. 1991. "Aristotle on Property Rights." In J. P. Anton and A. Preus, eds. *Essays in Ancient Greek Philosophy IV: Aristotle's Ethics*. Albany, N.Y.: State University of New York Press.

————. 1995. *Nature, Justice, and Rights in Aristotle's Politics*. Oxford: Oxford University Press.

Mulgan, R. G. 1977. *Aristotle's Political Theory*. Oxford: Oxford University Press.

Newman, W. L. 1887-1902. *The Politics of Aristotle*. 4 vols. Oxford: Clarendon Press.

Nichols, M. 1987. *Socrates and the Political Community: An Ancient Debate*. Albany, N.Y.: State University of New York Press.

Nussbaum, M. 1980. "Shame, Separateness, and Political Unity: Aristotle's Criticism of Plato." In Rorty (1980), 395-435.

————. 1988. "Nature, Function, and Capability: Aristotle on Political Distribution." *Oxford Studies in Ancient Greek Philosophy*. Supplementary Vol., 145-84 (with "Reply to David Charles," 207-14). Oxford: Oxford University Press.

————. 1990. "Aristotelian Social Democracy." In B. Douglass, G. Mara, and H. Richardson, eds. *Liberalism and the Good*. New York: Routledge.

Parker, R. 1983. *Miasma: Pollution and Purification in Early Greek Religion*. Oxford: Oxford University Press.

Patzig, G., ed. 1990. *Aristotles' "Politik": Akten des XI. Symposium Aristotelicum Friedrichshafen/Bodensee 25.8-3.9.1987*. Göttingen: Vandenhoeck and Ruprecht.

Popper, K. 1971. *The Open Society and Its Enemies*. Vol. 1. *The Spell of Plato*. 5th ed. Princeton: Princeton University Press.

Price, A. W. 1989. *Love and Friendship in Plato and Aristotle*. Oxford: Clarendon Press.

Reeve, C. D. C. 1988. *Philosopher-Kings: The Argument of Plato's Republic*. Princeton: Princeton University Press.

Rhodes, P. J. 1984. *Aristotle: The Athenian Constitution*. Harmondsworth, England: Penguin.

————. 1993. *A Commentary on the Aristotelian Athenaion Politeia*. 2nd ed. Oxford: Oxford University Press.

Rorty, A., ed. 1980. *Essays on Aristotle's Ethics*. Berkeley: University of California Press.

Ross, W. D. 1924. *Aristotle's Metaphysics*. 2 vols. Oxford: Clarendon Press.

————. 1957. *Aristotelis Politica*. Oxford: Oxford University Press.

Saunders, T. J. 1992. *Aristotle, The Politics*. Trans. T. A. Sinclair (1962), revised by Saunders (1981), reprinted with revised bibliography (1992). Harmondsworth, England: Penguin.

————. 1995. *Aristotle, Politics Books I and II*. Oxford: Clarendon Press.

Saxonhouse, A. W. 1982. "Family, Polity, and Unity: Aristotle on Socrates' Community of Wives." *Polity* 15: 202-19.

————. 1985. "The Net of Hephaestus: Aristophanes' Speech in Plato's *Symposium*." *Interpretation* 13: 15-32.

Schütrumpf, E. 1991. *Aristoteles Politik*. Vol. 2. Berlin: Akademie-Verlag.

Sealey, R. 1976. *A History of the Greek City States 700-338 B.C.* Berkeley: University of California Press.

Shorey, P. 1930. *Plato: The Republic*. 2 vols. Cambridge, Mass.: Harvard University Press

Simpson, P. 1991. "Aristotle's Criticisms of Socrates' Communism of Wives and Children." *Apeiron* 24: 99-113.

Smyth, H. W. 1956. *Greek Grammar*. 2nd ed. Cambridge, Mass.: Harvard University Press

Sorabji, R. 1980. *Necessity, Cause and Blame*. London: Duckworth.

————. 1990. "Comments on J. Barnes." In Patzig (1990), 264-76.

Stalley, R. F. 1991. "Aristotle's Criticism of Plato's *Republic*." In D. Keyt and F. D. Miller Jr., eds. *A Companion to Aristotle's Politics*, 182-99. Oxford: Basil Blackwell.

Strauss, L. 1978. *The City and Man*. 2nd ed. Chicago: University of Chicago Press.

Striker, G. 1990. "Comments on T. Irwin." In Patzig (1990), 99-100.

Susemihl, F., and R. D. Hicks. 1894. *The Politics of Aristotle, Books I-V*. London: Macmillan.

Szegedy-Maszak, A. 1987. *The Nomoi of Theophrastus*. Salem, N.H.: Ayer.

Ussher, R. G. 1960. *The Characters of Theophrastus*. London: Macmillan.

————. 1973. *Aristophanes, Ecclesiazusae*. Oxford: Oxford University Press.

Waldron, J. 1988. *The Right to Private Property*. Oxford: Clarendon Press.

Waterfield, R. 1994. *Plato: Republic*. Oxford: Oxford University Press.

Wycherly, R. E. 1976. *How the Greeks Built Their Cities*. 2nd ed. New York: Norton.

Yack, B. 1993. *The Problems of a Political Animal: Community, Justice, and Conflict in Aristotelian Political Thought*. Berkeley: University of California Press.

General Index

affection. *See* friendship
alliance (*summachia*), 14, 26-28, 32-33n2, 36n2, 82, 93n64
animals, 15-17, 20, 33-34n5, 64
aristocracy, 29, 81, 93n60
Aristotle as critic of Plato, reputation of, 1-2, 7, 8nn3-4, 11n16, 36n38, 37, 115n16, 124, 127n1, 129-30
Arkadia, 14, 32-33n2

business expertise (*chrēmatikē*), 43-44, 52, 56n25

Carthage, 4, 9n10
citizens, 5-6, 17, 22, 25-26, 28, 34n6, 34n17, 42, 44-46, 48, 53, 65, 72-73, 82-84, 88-89n30, 97, 107-8, 110, 112-13, 117n28, 120n52, 121n63, 126
city (*polis*), 10n14, 13-14, 17-20, 22, 25, 27-28, 31, 31n1, 35n18, 37-38, 40-48, 88-89n30, 108, 112-13, 117n31, 119n44, 121n63, 124; as natural, 18-19; parts of, 14, 17-18, 21, 25, 40-45, 51, 55n8, 81-82, 113, 121, 124-26; unity of, 2-3, 6, 13-16, 27-28, 30-31, 38, 51, 53, 59-60, 70-71, 83-85, 113-14, 120n52, 122n64, 125, 135
common meals (*sussitia*), 108-10, 117n28, 118n37, 120nn49-52
communism, Platonic, 5-8, 9-10n14, 11n16, 12n21, 13-14, 31, 31n1, 51-53, 59-61, 70-73, 79, 85, 86n4, 88n28, 91n44, 95-105, 113, 114n1,

114n6, 115n16, 116n24-25, 117n31, 118n33, 123-24, 129-35, 136n1, 137n5, 137n8
community (*koinōnia*), 3, 5, 10n15, 17-18, 20, 35n19. *See also* city *and* household
concord (*homonoia*), 61, 80-83, 93n62, 93-94n71. *See also* friendship
constitution (*politeia*), 3-5, 7, 9n12, 27-29, 34n7, 36nn33-34, 50, 81, 88-89n30, 95, 108, 122n64; best, 3-4, 81, 95, 108. *See also* city
Crete, 4, 9-10n10, 109-110, 120n49, 120n51
cyclopes, 19, 34n16

democracy, 29, 92n57
dialectic, 65, 87n17, 88n29, 88-89n30

education, 28, 35n18, 36n34, 47, 49, 79, 92n53, 102, 112-13, 117n28, 120n52, 121nn61-63, 122n64, 126
equality, 14, 19, 21-22, 26, 28-31, 35n26, 36n36, 45, 81, 92n59, 93n61, 97-98, 101. *See also* justice

favoritism, 63-64
freedom. *See* independence
friendship (*philia*), 59, 62-64, 68, 71-74, 81, 85, 85n1, 87n10, 90n42, 91n46, 93n63, 93n20, 104, 107-108, 113; types of: between cities, 27, 93n64; character, 74-77, 79, 82, 85, 91n45,

Index of Names

Index Locorum

About the Author

Robert Mayhew is assistant professor of philosophy at Seton Hall University. He earned an M.A. and Ph.D. from Georgetown University. He has published numerous articles and reviews on the moral and political philosophy of Plato and Aristotle, as well as a translation of Aristophanes' *Assembly of Women* (Buffalo, N.Y.: Prometheus Books, 1997). He is currently working on a book on Aristotle's views on women.

CPSIA information can be obtained at www.ICGtesting.com
Printed in the USA
LVOW05s1413200913

353406LV00001B/24/P